YUKON
COOKBOOK

LEONA KANANEN

DOUGLAS & McINTYRE
Vancouver

Canadian Shared Cataloguing in Publication Data

Kananen, Leona.
    Yukon cookbook

    Includes index.
    ISBN 0-88894-016-5 pa.

    1. Cookery (Wild foods). 2. Cookery, Canadian.
    3. Cookery (Sourdough). I. Title.
    TX715.K35   641.6

Douglas & McIntyre Ltd.
1615 Venables Street
Vancouver, British Columbia

Jacket design by Nancy Legue-Grout
Illustrations by Leona Kananen
Printed and bound in Canada

CONTENTS

Section 1

GAME
WILD FOWL
and
FISH

GAME
Moose

In the Yukon, moose is the most plentiful of game; it is the staple of diet in Yukon native cookery.

Many oldtimers prefer to cook moose with a minimum of seasoning and a small amount of water, so as not to destroy the moose flavor; this is best done with a young moose (which has been skillfully hunted and carefully cleaned!)

The person who has not acquired a taste for moose may wish to enhance, disguise, or get rid of the moose flavor entirely. This he can do by seasoning it; by parboiling or marinating it, and by combining it with certain other foods.

The following recipes represent different approaches to cooking moose meat.

MOOSE SHISH KEBOBS

Let the campfire burn down to a good bed of coals.

Cut tenderloin into 2-inch cubes.

Sharpen one end of a small stick which should be about a foot long.

Start with a piece of tenderloin and alternate with a small wild mushroom or piece of mushroom, taking care not to split the mushrooms, pushing each one onto the stick until it is full. End with a piece of meat, and have the mushroom and tenderloin close together.

Cook slowly over coals, brushing often with melted fat.

Information on dressing and cutting game meats may be obtained through the Yukon Game Branch.

PAUPIETTES DE MOOSE BISCOISE

2 pounds moose steak, cut ¼ inch thick
¼ cup unbleached flour
½ teaspoon salt
¼ teaspoon pepper, freshly ground
dash of sweet marjoram, rosemary and thyme
1 cup water
1½ cups sage dressing

Cut moose into 2- by 4-inch slices, and pound flour and seasonings well into each piece.

Place a mound of sage dressing in the center of each slice; fold meat over the stuffing and fasten with a toothpick.

Place meat in roaster, and bake in a moderate oven for 1 hour, letting it brown well before serving.

SAGE DRESSING

Break up dry or soft bread or oven bannock into rather large pieces about the size of a 25-cent piece. Average about 2 quarts of diced or broken bread for a medium roast of 5-7 pounds

Add sage or regular poultry seasoning and fluff through until the bread is covered with green dust. At least 1 large onion should be chopped up (not too small) and added along with additional seasoning, salt and pepper to taste. Some chopped celery is a nice addition. Sprinkle water throughout—until stuffing is quite moist.

If dry bread is used, a quick soaking in water is necessary in the beginning.

MOOSE RIBS

When moose is cooked this way, the natural flavor is retained.

Put all the ribs (best from a younger moose) in 2 layers. Season with salt and pepper, and slice onions over the top. Roast slowly in a covered pan. Check as they cook, and add a little water, just enough to steam them.

MOOSE ROAST WITH SAGE DRESSING

Heap sage dressing in the bottom of roasting pan. Cut moose roast to flatten out, and lay it over stuffing. Ribs are best, but this is also a way to make tasty use of the poorer cuts of meat.

Cover pan throughout cooking; about 2½ hours, or more if the meat is tough. Push meat aside and uncover for 20 minutes to slightly brown stuffing.

STUFFED MOOSE HEART

Spread heart open, and fill with stuffing. Roast slowly in oven with the lid on; uncover towards the end of cooking to brown it.

MOOSE SWISS STEAK

Cut moose round steak ¾ inch thick. Mix flour, salt, pepper and sage; pound as much of the seasoned flour as you can into the meat, using the edge of a saucer.

Heat frying pan with a little oil; brown meat on both sides. Transfer to roasting pan, and cover with 1 can of onion soup diluted with 1 can water.

Put into 300-350 F oven and let simmer for 1 hour.

Variation 1:
Omit onion soup. Add 1 cup tomato juice, 1 dash soy sauce, 1 stalk celery and 1 onion, sliced. Half a green bell pepper may also be added.

Variation 2:
Omit onion soup. Add 1 onion, sliced; 1 clove garlic, 2 cans stewed tomatoes and ½ pound mushrooms.

MARINATED RIBS OF MOOSE

Take side of moose ribs, 2 pieces about a foot wide.

Season lightly with garlic powder, about as much as you would use of pepper; rub well into meat.

Sprinkle generously with soy sauce, then with dark brown sugar, a good tablespoon of sugar to each piece. Shake seasoned salt liberally over this, and rub seasonings in on both sides.

Stack pieces of meat together as tight as possible. Slip into a plastic bag, pressing out air. Fold up tightly and leave for 36 hours in the refrigerator.

After the first 12 hours, remove meat from bag and rub accumulated liquid back into meat. Place in bag and pack tightly. Wine, about 2 ounces for 5 pounds of meat, can be added. Bake ribs in the oven, or barbecue over a campfire.

QUICK MOOSE ROAST

1 moose roast
½ teaspoon nutmeg
½ teaspoon onion powder
Beef fat slices, enough to cover roast

Clean roast and sprinkle top with nutmeg, onion powder, and salt and pepper to taste.

Tie or skewer slices of beef fat onto roast to cover.

Put into roasting pan and pour water into the pan. Roast in 375 F oven until done. (You may like to use the drippings to make Yorkshire Pudding and gravy.)

MOOSE POT ROAST WITH VEGETABLES

Coat roast well with flour, and brown in fat in dutch oven about 20 minutes, or until browned all over.

Pour 2 cups vegetable broth, water, or other liquid over meat; cover, and cook in a slow oven, or over a slow fire for 2-3½ hours, or until fork-tender. Baste occasionally.

Whole peeled carrots, potatoes, a stalk of celery and whole onion may be added during the last hour. Thicken gravy with 1 tablespoon flour mixed with ½ cup water, and season to taste.

7

ROAST MOOSE

The parboiling leaves you a roast that tastes very much like roast beef.

Boil moose in water to cover, with ½ cup vinegar added, for 20 minutes. This will take away most of the "wild" taste.

Clean roast well with cold water. Make deep cuts about 2 inches apart all over the roast, cutting almost to the bottom. Give the knife a twist to make an opening; pour cooking oil into each hole.

Sprinkle roast with liberal amount of seasoning to taste: sage, poultry seasoning, bay leaf powder, garlic, etc.

Cover roast with sliced onions, then with strips of fat, or with bacon.

Bake on a rack in a roasting pan with a little water in it, and with the oven set at 300-325 F. Roast until tender, approximately 35 minutes to a pound. To test, poke it with a fork, if the tines go in and come out easily, it's done.

MOOSE ROAST DELUXE

Wipe roast well and season with the following spices:
  1½ teaspoons allspice
  1 teaspoon dry mustard
  1 teaspoon oregano
  1 teaspoon marjoram
  1 tablespoon brown sugar
  salt to taste
  garlic if you wish
Rub spices well into meat.

Sprinkle all over with ½ cup wine. Let stand for 1 hour in a shallow pan, turning meat from time to time so that both sides are saturated. Remove the meat, saving the remaining wine.

Dredge meat in flour and sear in heavy cast iron frying pan. When roast is browned on all sides, transfer to baking pan and bake in a slow oven until the meat is tender and well done, usually 2-4 hours. The time will depend on texture and size of meat. A half hour before the meat is done, add the wine mixture. This makes a good gravy.

SUET GRAVY

4 tablespoons beef fat
2 tablespoons flour
2 cups milk, soup stock, or water
salt and pepper to taste

Melt beef fat; blend in flour until a smooth paste is formed. Add liquid gradually, very slowly at first, stirring constantly until smooth. Keep stirring until the flour is well cooked and the gravy thickens, about 10 minutes; then it may be set aside and left until time to serve.

BARBECUED MOOSE

Method 1:
Tie roast with a cord and hang it above a fire. Wind the cord tight, so that when you let it go, the roast turns. After a while, when it has stopped turning, wind it up again, or turn the roast with a stick. This makes a very tender roast.

Method 2:
Wash stomach well; fill pouch with brisket and other meats; tie above a fire. Turn meat while it's cooking.

MOOSE ROAST

This is done with a frozen moose roast.

Drop the unthawed roast into a roaster pan and sprinkle with salt and pepper. Put a little water and half a medium or large onion, sliced, into the bottom of the pan. Cover roast with lid or with tin foil, and roast long and slowly.

MOOSE MULLIGAN

Usually the brisket, rib or rump is used.

Cut meat into fairly large pieces, and put into a pot with enough water to cover. Boil for 3 minutes over an open campfire; then simmer slowly for 30 minutes.

After 30 minutes add any vegetables you have. Onions, turnips and carrots must be added first; potatoes, 15 minutes later. Add rice. Allow 20 minutes for white or converted rice, and 45 minutes for brown rice. Tomatoes may be used if you have them.

Every once in a while, twist the pot with jerky clockwise movements of the wrist, being careful not to burn yourself. When meat and vegetables are tender, remove from heat and serve.

BARBECUED MOOSE

Combine:
>   1 cup salad oil
>   ½ cup onions, finely chopped
>   ½ cup brown sugar
>   1 cup lemon juice or vinegar
>   2 cups tomato paste
>   2 tablespoons Worcestershire sauce
>   1 teaspoon salt
>   1 teaspoon paprika
>   1 teaspoon chili powder
>   1 cup water

Simmer sauce over a slow fire for 1 hour.

Sprinkle meat (either steaks, roasts or ribs) with meat tenderizer and seasoning salt, or salt. Brush with sauce, and barbecue over hot coals, brushing with sauce periodically.

BAKED MOOSE

This method keeps the seasoning and the moisture sealed in.

Lard meat, and rub well with garlic and either 4 whole allspice berries or a few crushed juniper berries.

Sprinkle with ½-1 cup red wine and 2 tablespoons maple syrup or brown sugar. Add 1 large onion, sliced, and 1 or 2 bay leaves. Marinate for several days in the refrigerator, turning frequently. Remove roast, and discard marinade.

Take 3 sheets of brown grocery paper and thoroughly saturate them with oil. Lay 1 sheet over the roast.

With a thick paste of flour and water, coat the sheet of paper which is lying over the roast. Lay the other 2 sheets over this, and wrap securely around roast. Tie with string or dental floss.

Bake at 325 F about 35 minutes to a pound.

During the last ½ hour of cooking, crack open the dried-out paste, and discard. Baste roast generously with butter, dust lightly with flour, return to oven and bake until golden brown.

MOOSE POT ROAST

Cut meat into 2- or 3-inch chunks, and dredge in flour with seasonings to taste. Brown quickly in a hot oven or under broiler; then put into a dutch oven or casserole with a little water, and cook slowly until tender. Vegetables may be added the last 45 minutes or hour of cooking.

HUNTER'S STEW

>   moose, deer or caribou in 1½-inch cubes
>   potatoes, fresh or dehydrated
>   onions
>   carrots

Sear meat, and cook with vegetables over medium heat. When fully cooked, add flour and water thickener, salt and pepper, 1 tablespoon Worcestershire sauce, and Yukon mushrooms if available. You can also add bannock or dumplings.

MOOSE MEAT HASH

Mix together:
>   2-3 cups leftover cooked rice
>   1 can tomatoes
>   ½ pound leftover moose meat in small pieces
>   ¼-½ teaspoon sage
>   1 clove garlic, crushed

Heat thoroughly in skillet or in oven; add salt, pepper and onion powder to taste.

YUKON STEW

Mix some flour with seasonings to taste.

Cut about 2 pounds moose round steak into 1-inch pieces, and roll it in the flour to coat well.

Brown meat lightly, and scrape into a kettle. Add:

1 tablespoon Worcestershire
    sauce
2 onions, sliced
1 can tomatoes

Cook over a slow fire until tender, or 1½-2 hours. Mushrooms may be added during the last ½ hour to 5 minutes before serving.

The stew may be varied by substituting 1 cup water for tomatoes, and in the last hour of cooking adding sliced carrots and celery and cut-up potatoes.

MOOSE PATTIES

1½ pounds ground moose
1½ cups bread crumbs
½ cup celery, finely chopped
1 egg, slightly beaten
½ cup water
1½ teaspoons salt
½ teaspoon sage, or poultry
    seasoning

Sauté celery in 2 tablespoons butter for 10 minutes, and add the remaining ingredients. Mix thoroughly, and shape into patties or balls about 1 inch in diameter. Brown both sides in butter, then lower heat and cook 10 minutes. Pour onion gravy over the patties and simmer gently for a few minutes.

ONION GRAVY

Blend 2 tablespoons butter and 1½ tablespoons flour in skillet. Stir and cook until lightly browned. Add 1 cup water gradually, until mixture is smooth and thickened; stir constantly. Add 1 cup onions, thinly sliced, and 1 cup finely shredded lettuce; cook over low heat with the cover on for 15 minutes.

MOOSE MEAT SPANISH RICE

2½ cups short grain brown rice,
    cooked
8 ounces mixed vegetable juice,
    fresh or canned, or tomato
    juice
¾ pound ground moose meat
1 tablespoon salad oil, or fresh
    rendered bacon fat
½ teaspoon cumin
½ teaspoon oregano
½ teaspoon basil
¼ cup celery, chopped
1 onion, minced
1 bell pepper, minced
1 clove garlic, crushed
paprika

Sauté onion, bell pepper, celery and ground moose meat in oil or bacon fat for about 10 minutes.

Add juice and cook until hot; stir in rice, oregano, basil, cumin and paprika and gently heat through until hot.

MOOSE OR CARIBOU TONGUE

1 moose or caribou tongue
2 quarts water
1 teaspoon onion juice
2 cloves
1 teaspoon parsley
2 tablespoons butter
1 onion
1 tablespoon flour
1 tablespoon lemon juice
1 bay leaf
2 tablespoons seedless raisins
2 tablespoons honey
1 tablespoon vinegar

Soak tongue overnight.

Place tongue in kettle with water, onion juice, cloves and parsley. Simmer until tender; remove from liquid, and peel off skin. Strain 2 cups of the broth.

Melt butter in skillet; add onion; add flour and cook until flour is browned. Stir. Add the 2 cups of broth, lemon juice, bay leaf, raisins, honey and vinegar. Add tongue cut into slices, cover, and simmer 25 minutes.

MOOSE STEAK

Pound steaks well.

Dredge in flour; season to taste; fry in fresh butter with plenty of sliced onion and mushrooms. Sprinkle with minced parsley and serve.

If the steak is not choice, it may be marinated in milk for 12-24 hours; this will tenderize it, and take away any undesired flavors. Powdered milk diluted with evaporated milk or sour milk may be used.

BRAISED MOOSE STEAK

Place steak in pan with a little oil and enough water to half cover. Simmer slowly until the water has evaporated and the meat is done.

MOOSE STEAK SHISH KEBOBS

Cut steaks into 1½-inch cubes. Marinate in French dressing with sliced onions for 24 hours in the refrigerator. Spear on metal skewers or on green sticks, and broil in oven or over an open fire.

MOOSE STEAK IN TIN FOIL

Lay steak over a piece of tin foil; sprinkle with garlic powder and/or onion powder. Top with sliced onion and slices of mushroom (if available) and drained canned tomatoes (optional). Wrap securely and roast over hot coals or in a moderately hot oven for 1-2 hours.

MOOSE LIVER WITH LEMON

Dredge liver in flour seasoned with salt and pepper.

Heat fat in pan and brown liver on one side. Squeeze over it the juice of ½-1 lemon, according to the amount of liver. Turn and brown on the other side. Lower heat and let sit until done.

MOOSE TRIPE

Wash and peel tripe. Simmer until tender; cool, and cut into small squares. Add salt, vinegar, and chopped onion.

MOOSE STEAK AND KIDNEYS

1½ pounds moose round steak,
   cut into cubes
¼ pound moose kidney
3 tablespoons oil
3 tablespoons flour
3 tablespoons butter or
   bacon fat
seasoning to taste
2 cups stock
stew vegetables (optional)

Cut out the dark center part of the kidney. Saute kidney in the oil for 1 minute on each side, and discard oil.

Soak kidney for 2 hours in cold salted water.

Remove kidney and place in a pot with enough fresh water to cover; add 1 tablespoon vinegar, and simmer 15-20 minutes. Plunge kidney into cold water; drain, dry, and cut into ½-inch pieces.

Dredge steak and kidney in flour; season to taste.

Melt the butter, and brown the meat lightly. Simmer very slowly 1½ hours, until tender.

MOOSE AND SAUERKRAUT SOUP

1-2 pounds moose stew meat
   or hamburger
2 onions, chopped
4 or 5 potatoes, diced
1 carrot, diced
1 pound sauerkraut
butter

Brown onions and stew meat (not the hamburger) in butter; add water and onions; simmer slowly for about 3 hours; add potatoes and carrots the last 45 minutes.

Rinse sauerkraut if less sour flavor is desired; add to soup just before serving time.

MOOSE MEAT BARLEY SOUP

1 or 2 pounds moose stew meat,
cut into cubes
1 or 2 onions, chopped
4 or 5 potatoes, diced
about 1 cup barley

Brown onions and meat in oil or butter
or in the oven; add water, potatoes
and barley; simmer over low heat for
3 hours, or until meat is tender. Season
to taste.

MOOSE SOUP

If you want to make the most of your
moose, try this recipe from a back-
woods cook.

Simmer the bones and meat in
enough water for a soup, until the
meat begins to fall away from the
bone. Season to taste with your choice
of any of the following ingredients:

    tomato juice
    tomato paste
    canned tomatoes
    green onions, chopped
    celery, chopped
    Tabasco sauce
    Worcestershire sauce
    garlic
    salt
    parsley, minced
    paprika

MOOSE BRAWN

Take moose heart, tongue, soup bones
and leftover meat trimmings.

Simmer meat until it is tender,
using 3-4 quarts water to about 3
pounds meat.

Remove meat from broth, trim-
ming all bones, and chop into bite-
sized pieces.

Strain the broth. Boil it down, so
that you have about a quart for every
3 pounds of meat. Season to taste
with salt, pepper, and sage, or poultry
seasoning. A dash of allspice, dried
vegetable powder or flakes, or a few
onion flakes could also be used.

Soften some gelatin in a little cold
water for 5 minutes, using 2 tablespoons for each quart of broth that
you have.

Put the chopped meat back into the
pot along with the softened gelatin;
simmer for 15 minutes. Pour into
molds and chill until firm. Serve in
slices.

JELLIED MOOSE LOAF

1 tongue, either moose, caribou
or beef
pork hocks*
1 package gelatin

Boil tongue gently over slow heat for
about 3 hours, or until tender.

Boil hocks until meat falls from
bones, and save the broth.

Peel tongue while still warm; chop
meat into small pieces and place in a
loaf pan.

Dissolve gelatin in the broth. Season
with onion powder, garlic salt, pepper,
salt or any of your favorite seasonings.
A dash of allspice, dried vegetable
powder or flakes, sage or poultry
seasoning may also be used.

*Moose hooves, singed over a fire and
cleaned, may be used in the place of pork
hocks.

MOOSE MEAT
POTATO SAUSAGE

3 pounds ground moose
4 large potatoes, cooked and
mashed
1½ teaspoons salt
¼ teaspoon garlic powder
¼ teaspoon cinnamon
1 teaspoon sage
4 cups broth (made with onions)

Mix ingredients thoroughly, and run
mixture through a meat grinder, using
a fine disc.

The sausage may be made into
patties, rolled in flour and fried. Or it
may be stuffed into butcher's casings,
tied, and simmered in water to cover.

MOOSE JERKY
(OVEN DRIED)

2½-3 pounds round steak, cut
    2 inches thick
2 large onions, finely chopped
2 teaspoons oregano or sage
2 cloves garlic, mashed
2 teaspoons salt
½ teaspoon pepper
Trim and discard all fat and gristle.
    Slice meat thinly, 1/8 inch, across grain.

Place meat in a large crock or bowl, spreading onion and sprinkling seasoning over each layer; cover and chill at least overnight, or up to 24 hours.

Arrange meat in shallow pan (fills 3 pans, 10 inches by 15) or stretch the meat directly over the oven racks, allowing the meat to touch but not overlap.

Let the meat dry at 200 F for 6-7 hours or at 150 F for 11 hours or overnight, until it is dry and hard.

Remove meat from oven; cool; store in airtight bags or jars.

CANNED MOOSE MEAT
(COLD PACK METHOD)

Season meat to taste with salt, etc.

Pack meat into jars, and fill with cold water to within ½ inch from the top. Run a knife along the edges of the jar to release the air, then add more water if necessary so that it is an inch from top.

Seal jars and submerge in a boiler. Bring to a boil and simmer for 3½ hours. This method makes a tender and tasty meat.

(HOT PACK METHOD)

Cook meat over low heat for 2½ hours; season to taste, and seal in sterilized jars.

BOILED MOOSE

Put meat into a moosehide bag with water and a very hot, smooth, round rock.

ROAST MOOSE STRIP

Cut meat into long slices, and wind it around a long, green stick. Tie with snare wire, and cook.

DRIED MOOSE MEAT

The meat is cut into sheets, about ½ inch thick. If you see how it's done, then it's much easier. You can sprinkle it with salt if you want to.

Hang the sheets over pole to dry in the wind and sun, with a fire going underneath to keep the flies away.

MOOSE HEART

Boil heart in water; add onion, sage, salt and pepper; cook slowly until tender.

MOOSE HEAD

Skin head and take off horns. Hang by cord or chain over a fire, for 6 hours. Use a stick to turn meat as it roasts.

Another way to cook moose head is to just throw it into the fire; after it is cooked the skin is taken off.

MOOSE VELVET

(This can only be made early in the spring, when the antlers are in velvet.) Singe hairs off. Cut velvet into strips with knife, and bake over the fire.

INSTANT MOOSE

Take dried steak meat (very dry); put it onto a board and pound it until you get a stringy kind of powder. You may pound a little home-dried onion into it if you wish. Put it into a bone-dry jar, and keep on a shelf in a dry place. Three heaping tablespoons of this is the equivalent of a pound of meat.

When you come in from the bush tired and hungry, throw 3 tablespoons instant moose into the frying pan; add 4-5 cups water, and in no time you will have a thick sludge.

Instant moose keeps indefinitely.

SMOKED MOOSE MEAT

Build a slow, smoky fire of willow, or any wood that doesn't have pitch.

Put water into a large pot, and salt it heavily; boil for 5 minutes.

Take moose round steak about 2 inches thick, and slice very thin across the grain.

Tie cord around the strips of meat and dip each piece into salt water for 1-2 minutes.

Hang the meat from poles over the smoke, and leave for a minimum of 2 days, preferably 6-8 days, until it is dry and hard.

FRIED MOOSE STEAK

Look for 2 flat rocks. Put the rocks into ashes, and build a fire right over the rocks.

When you think the rocks are hot enough, wipe each one clean; rub one rock with grease, place the steak on it and cover the steak with the other rock, which is also greased; it will sizzle.

Do not use rocks which have been lying in or near water. Water-soaked rocks could explode when heated!

BOILED MOOSE NOSE

This is a delicacy.

Build a fire. Singe the nose in the flames with a wire suspending it, or by holding it on a long fork. Scrape, and singe again, repeating singeing and scraping until all the hairs are off. Roll up pieces of paper tightly, and light the ends to singe the hairs in the nostrils. Pull all the burn off, and boil for 3-4 hours. It is good hot or cold.

MOOSE TRIPE SAUSAGE

Use tenderloin of moose, either cut into slices or in one solid piece. Season with onion and with seasonings to taste.

Take the tripe (tubular part of stomach) and turn inside out. Wrap tenderloin in the tripe casing, tie both ends to seal, and boil until tripe is well done.

PEMMICAN

Best made in August.
First dry the meat:

Cut meat into strips and hang over a pole over a slow fire of dry willow; keep turning meat until well dried and smoked.

Cook meat in boiling water for 10 minutes. Pound well with hammer or axe, and mix with marrow or grease. Add chopped onions or berries, if you like. Put pemmican into packages, into a pan or into a moose stomach. Freeze; cut into slices.

MOOSE LIVER

Roll the liver in clay and bury it under a fire, in hot ashes; let it cook for about an hour, depending on how hot the coals are.

MOOSE LIVER SOUP

This is made only at running time, starting in September, when the liver turns white. At this time the liver can be sliced and broken up easily.

Boil a moose bone in water. Add the liver, which has been worked in the hands to a mush. Keep stirring until it boils, then blend in some rendered fat.

BOILED MOOSE HOOVES

Singe off hairs and clean.

Boil in water for several hours until meat falls from bone. When chilled, it's just like head cheese.

You can do the same with the sinews from the leg of the moose.

ROASTED MOOSE HOOVES

Singe off hairs, and clean. Roast hooves by the side of the fire.

Dall Sheep

BARBECUED SHEEP RIBS

Brush ribs with barbecue sauce or with soy sauce, or rub with a little garlic. Broil or barbecue 10-15 minutes on each side, brushing often with the sauce.

MOUNTAIN SHEEP BUMPER

Between the horns of the mountain sheep, at the back of the neck, is the bumper. Oldtimers know that this is a choice part. It can be roasted, but the preferred method of cooking it is to simmer it and chill it; sometimes in addition it is barbecued to brown the surface.

BARBECUED STEAK

Marinate steak in soy sauce with a clove of garlic.
    Leave steak in one piece and broil or barbecue in broiler or over a campfire. Or cut steak into chunks about 1½ inches square, and skewer on green sticks or on metal skewers; broil or barbecue the same.

MOUNTAIN SHEEP STEAKS

Dredge steak lightly in flour, and brown in cooking oil, or whatever you have handy. Add onions and mushrooms if desired.

BROILED DALL SHEEP CHOPS

Rub chops with garlic and/or marjoram; broil at least 5 inches from flame, turning often.

ROAST DALL SHEEP

Rub roast with garlic; roast in oven or on rotary barbecue at 325 F, 25-30 minutes per pound.

SHEEP STEW

Cut meat into 2-inch cubes, and simmer for 1½ hours with sliced carrots, sliced onions, celery, a pinch of marjoram, and enough stock or water to fill the pan ½ inch. Thicken gravy with flour and a little cold water; taste for salt.

BARBECUED ROAST OF MOUNTAIN SHEEP

Hang the roast over a slow fire, using a long cord or chain. When the cord is wound tightly and then released, the roast is turned as if cooked on a rotisserie. Keep winding the cord every so often, or give it a turn with a stick. The roast will be tender and juicy when done this way.

Mountain Goat

ROAST MOUNTAIN GOAT

    5-6 pound roast
    1 or 2 cloves garlic
Thoroughly clean meat; then make small openings with the point of a sharp knife and insert small pieces of garlic.
    Put into roaster with a small amount of water. Brown quickly in a hot oven. Then roast in a slow oven, 20-25 minutes per pound, or until tender.
    Serve with cranberry catsup made from high bush cranberries.

ROAST SHEEP or GOAT

Rub roast with a little garlic, onion and seasoning salt. Wrap in parchment paper, either oiled or soaked in water, then wrap in 2 or 3 layers of wet newspaper. Put onto hot coals, cover with an old metal pan or with green leaves, and let cook for at least 24 hours.

Caribou

Bear

ROAST CARIBOU or MOOSE

At night, when you're camping out, build a good fire. Make a hole for the roast. Put a few logs on, and let them smolder away.

Take a chunk of caribou, a good-sized roast; wash it; put on some salt and pepper, and onions if you like.

To seal in the moisture, wrap the roast in oiled brown paper.

Wash a burlap or gunny sack well in water; rinse; wrap the sack around the paper. This will keep the paper from burning. Then wrap the burlap in heavy tin foil.

Put a few hot coals in the bottom of the hole; place the roast over them and bury with hot ashes.

In the morning, take the roast out; it will be tender and juicy.

SPICED, BRAISED CARIBOU or MOOSE

(3 pounds lean meat)
Place meat in a crock or in a casserole with lid; cover with a mixture of:

    1 teaspoon salt
    1 teaspoon pepper
    1 tablespoon dry mustard
    ½ teaspoon thyme
    ½ teaspoon sage
    1 cup dry red wine, or tomato
       juice

Place in refrigerator and turn daily for 1 week.

Remove meat and brown in 500 F oven for 15 minutes; reduce heat to 300 F and add:

    1 cup cooked, chopped
       mushrooms
    1 tablespoon tomato paste

Cook until reduced to 2 cups of gravy. Serve with meat. (4 servings.)

Any beef recipe can be used for bear meat, but be certain to cook it thoroughly as for pork.

BEAR STEAK

The bear should be young and tender.

Rub steak with sliced onion and spread generously with butter; sprinkle with salt and pepper. Broil in a hot oven, turning frequently. Cook at least 20 minutes per pound. Bear meat, when cooked, should be treated as pork.

ROAST BEAR

Trim off fat. Parboil roast over a slow flame for ½-1 hour (this draws out excess fat).

Remove roast and lay on a rack in a roasting pan. Insert slits of garlic all over if desired.

Put meat into a preheated, hot (450 F) oven to brown. Turn heat down shortly to medium-slow (335 F) and roast 35-40 minutes per pound.

BRAISED BROWN BEAR

(3-pound roast)
Trim off all fat right away, and cut meat into chunks about 2 or 3 inches square. Cover with water, and simmer slowly for about ½ hour.

Marinate in 2 cups tomato juice for 24 hours. (Use wine if you prefer.)

Remove meat; pat dry, and rub well with garlic. Dredge in flour, and brown on all sides in a dutch oven, using about 2 tablespoons oil, butter, or bacon fat.

Add 1 onion, stuck with 3 whole allspice or 2 whole cloves; 1 carrot, sliced; 1 stalk celery, sliced; 2 cups water and 1 cup seasoned broth or tomato juice. Cover and simmer slowly until tender, about 3-4 hours. Add whole peeled carrots or bear root, and whole potatoes if desired, during the last hour of cooking.

SMALL GAME

ROAST YUKON HARE or SNOWSHOE RABBIT

Skin and clean rabbit, taking special care not to puncture the bladder.

Place in a roasting pan, and cross the hind legs. Season with onion, salt and pepper, and cover with fat. Roast very slowly with the cover on, for 3 hours. To brown, turn heat up and remove cover the last ½ hour or so of cooking.

YUKON HARE COOKED IN SOUR CREAM

Any game or wild fowl may be prepared in this way:

Salt and pepper meat, and dredge with flour; brown with butter in a heavy dutch oven. Add sour cream and simmer until cream is fairly brown.

Add milk to cover, and simmer until done. Ten minutes before serving stir in 1 teaspoon vinegar and 1 teaspoon brown sugar; thicken gravy with flour.

STEWED HARE or RABBIT WITH BANNOCK DUMPLINGS

1 rabbit, cleaned and cut into
    serving-sized portions
1¾ cups water
¾ teaspoon salt
1 small onion, in thin slices
1 carrot, sliced
2 stalks celery, sliced
3 tablespoons flour
½ cup water or broth
    or 1 cup sour cream
pinch dried sage
paprika
bannock dough

Put rabbit, water, salt, onion, carrot and celery into pot; simmer 1 hour or longer, until meat is tender. If you wish, you may then remove the meat from the bone and return it to the pot.

Stir flour into ½ cup water or broth (or 1 cup of sour cream) and shake or beat until smooth. Add this to the rabbit along with the sage. Sprinkle with a little paprika, and taste for salt. Add a dab of butter if desired.

Bring to a simmer, and lay spoonfuls of bannock dough over the top. Cover with a close-fitting lid, and cook for 15 minutes, or until bannock is done.

FRIED HARE or RABBIT

Method 1:
Cut rabbit in half, or in sections. Roll in a little flour and fry slowly in fat on all sides. Drain and serve.

Method 2:
Clean rabbit; wash, and soak in salt water overnight.

Wash rabbit again the next morning, then put into a pot with enough water to cover, ¼ bay leaf, and the juice of ½ lemon; boil gently until tender.

Drain rabbit on paper towelling.

In a pan mix flour and salt. Roll rabbit in flour; fry in hot fat until golden brown. Allow 1 rabbit per person.

September is the best month for fresh rabbit; by November it begins to have a piney taste.

STEWED PORCUPINE

Put porcupine into a good fire to burn off the quills.

Scrape, then peel the skin off; clean; then boil porcupine in water, enough to cover. Change the water and boil with seasoning to taste, until tender.

GOPHER

You may singe all the fur off, or skin the gopher.

Clean gopher. Cut it into 4 parts, split it in half, or leave it whole. It can be roasted on a stick over a fire, or in the oven; or it can be boiled.

BAKED GOPHER

1 medium-sized gopher
1 medium-sized onion
12 whole cloves
salt and pepper to taste
½ cup water
½ can tomato soup
Combine all ingredients in a casserole and bake in a 300 F oven for 3 hours.

BEAVER TAIL

Roast beaver tail over campfire, cut it open and pull the skin off. (This makes a very rich meat.)

PICKLED BEAVER PAWS

Cook beaver paws slowly in water with a little vinegar added, until meat begins to fall from bones. Season to taste with salt, onion, bay leaf or other seasoning. Chill, or seal in sterilized jars. The same can be done with bear paws.

ROAST BEAVER

Clean beaver, and strip off all fat, including scent glands. Soak in water to cover with ¼ cup vinegar, overnight.

Wash meat; pat dry, and place on rack in a roasting pan; add ¼ cup water. Brush roast with butter; cover, and bake in a moderate oven.

Take off the cover when the roast is half cooked; add a cup of vegetables, finely chopped: onion, celery, and carrots. Finish cooking with the lid off, adding more water if necessary until the meat begins to fall from the bones.

POT ROASTED GROUND SQUIRREL

Trap, snare or shoot squirrels, but let shot hit head only. Skin them, being careful not to take off too much of the fat; then clean stomach; cut off head and feet.

Cut into pieces and shake in a bag of flour, as you do with chicken. Brown in deep fat. When brown, add boiling water and simmer 10 minutes.

Add onion, a pinch of wild sage, salt, and potatoes if you wish. Cook until tender; make sure gravy doesn't get too thick.

The same recipe may be used for hoary marmot or muskrat.

When cleaning muskrat remove the musk glands which lie on the underside of the body and cut away all fat. Parboil in salted water to cover, for 15 minutes, before preparing the dish.

SQUIRREL

Yukoners seldom eat squirrel as a preference, but it is used as an emergency food.

Squirrels can be cooked successfully by using any good recipe for chicken. Younger squirrels can be fried, broiled or roasted; older squirrels need to be simmered or braised.

STUFFED MUSKRAT

Chop into bite-sized pieces whatever vegetables desired: carrots, onions, potatoes, even green peppers—they make good flavoring. Add salt, seasoned salt or pepper to taste. Stuff muskrat.

Roast at 300-350 F for 15 minutes, turn oven down to 250 F, and roast for 2½-3 hours. Or roast at 350 F for 1 hour or longer; baking at low temperature for long hours makes it more tender. Add a little water, about ½ cup, to keep it moist. It's best to leave the fat on while cooking; cut it off before serving if you don't like to eat fat.

WILD FOWL

ROAST WILD DUCK

Clean the duck as soon as it is retrieved, removing crop, innards and intestines.

Hang duck by feet in a cool, dry, airy place for 24-48 hours.

Pluck feathers from duck, including all pin feathers, using tweezers, or forefinger and the tip of a knife. It helps to singe the bird first: Hold duck by legs and pass it quickly through a blue flame (candle, gas or campfire).

Check carefully for shot and dog-damaged areas. Remove the oil sac from the base of the tail.

Rub duck with salt. Fill cavity with dressing, and bake in a preheated, 350 F oven, uncovered, 30 minutes per pound, basting every 5 minutes.

STUFFING

(For 2 large mallards or 4 small teal.)
    ½ cup butter
    ¼ teaspoon each powdered sage,
        rosemary, thyme and marjoram
    1 teaspoon salt
    1 cup green onions, coarsely
        sliced, green tops included
    1 cup celery, coarsely chopped,
        some center leaves included
    1 cup parsley, coarsely chopped
    2 cups dry bread, crumbled
Mix ingredients well. Lightly salt cavities of birds and stuff with dressing.

FRUIT STUFFING

Stuff each duck with a mixture of 2 apples, cut into quarters; ½ cup raisins and orange juice. Baste frequently with orange juice.

GOOSE BAKED IN MUD

Clean goose and chop off legs and neck; leave feathers on. Salt inside, and tie goose around to hold in wings.

Make a big ball of mud around goose, and lay this in a nest of hot coals; build a good-sized fire over it, and let it cook for 1 hour. To break open casing, insert a knife into it, and bang knife with a rock or log. The feathers will be pulled off with the clay.

ROAST WILD GOOSE

    1 wild goose
    ½ cup butter
    ½ cup orange juice,
        fresh or frozen
    3 juniper berries
Draw, hang, pluck and singe goose, same as for wild duck.

Rub cavity of goose with salt and pepper.

Roast for 3 hours at 325 F. Baste frequently with orange juice, juniper berries and ¼ cup water. Prick lightly all over to allow fat to drain off.

Prepare dressing in a separate pan to keep it free from excessive fat and wild flavor.

BREAD STUFFING FOR DUCK or GOOSE

(Enough for 3 ducks or 1 goose.)
    Dried bread crumbs, enough to
        fill a 2-quart bowl
    1 large onion, chopped
    2 apples, chopped
    salt and pepper
    summer savory
Combine ingredients; pour over them just enough boiling water to soak the bread, so that it is slightly soggy.

BREAST OF YUKON GROUSE WITH DRESSING

Skin grouse and cut breast meat from bone.

Prepare in a paper bag a mixture of salt, pepper and flour. Shake meat in this mixture until well coated.

Brown meat in oil or bacon grease in a heavy dutch oven or skillet.

Prepare a bread stuffing as you would for chicken, only add a little more sage. Form this into small balls about 1 inch in diameter.

Add a little water to meat in skillet. Place dressing balls on top of meat; cover tightly and simmer 1½ hours on low heat.

GROUSE BAKED IN FOIL

Cut grouse into halves, and place on a sheet of foil; rub with lemon juice and season with salt and pepper; sprinkle with garlic powder and wrap securely.

Cook in hot coals for ½ hour, or in a 350 F oven for 1 hour.

BLUE GROUSE

Treat exactly as you would a very good chicken: stuff with sage dressing and roast.

BAKED BREASTS OF GROUSE or PTARMIGAN

Skin breasts and soak in milk overnight. (This will cut any excessively gamey flavor.)

Pat meat dry; dredge with flour, and brown on both sides in melted butter.

Place in shallow casserole. Season to taste with salt, pepper and paprika. Dot with butter, and cover with sliced onions. Add ½ cup sour cream, 1 teaspoon Worcestershire sauce and 1 teaspoon celery seed. Cover and bake at 325 F for 2 hours.

SAGE DRESSING

½ cup onion, chopped
¼-½ cup celery, chopped
1 cup mushrooms, sliced
   (optional)
¼ cup parsley, minced
1 clove garlic, crushed
½ bell pepper
2-4 cups day-old bread,
   without crusts
½ teaspoon paprika
½ teaspoon sage, or
   1 teaspoon poultry seasoning
¾ teaspoon salt, or to taste
1-2 cups boiling water

Either steam the onion, celery, mushrooms, parsley, garlic and bell pepper in ¼ cup of the water, or saute them in a few tablespoons butter; about 5 minutes. Add bread crumbs, seasonings and enough water to moisten.

WILD RICE DRESSING

1 cup wild rice
1 teaspoon salt
1 quart boiling water
½-1 cup mushrooms, sliced
2 tablespoons grated onion
¼ cup celery, finely chopped
½ teaspoon sage
¼ cup tomato paste (optional)

Wash rice well and stir into the boiling water; add salt, and cook slowly until tender, about 40 minutes.

Sauté mushrooms, onions and celery in butter for 5 minutes. Combine with rice, sage, and (if you wish) tomato paste; heat thoroughly and serve.

FISH

SMOKED SALMON

Make a fire of willow, and get it burning so that it's smoky and not too hot.
Cut salmon at least 1-1½ inches thick. When it's too thin it's no good.
Hang over pole, and let it smoke for at least 6 days.
To keep salmon, skin it, slice it, and let it dry.

PICNIC FISH

Take a fresh, whole fish.
Clean fish and sprinkle inside cavity with salt.
Wrap in lots of newspaper. Dip the whole package in water, so that the paper is thoroughly saturated.
Bury under hot coals (not a fire) and leave 25-30 minutes per pound of fish. To serve, cut paper open; the skin will come right off with the paper.

SALMON BAKE

The first thing you have to do is to dig a pit according to the size of your fish, about 3 feet deep and 6 feet in length. Line pit with stones or bricks, leaving a space in the center for the fish. Build a roaring big fire; keep it going until it burns right down to coals.
Take any size fish; clean well and remove head.
Wrap fish in foil (or use a well washed old shirt or cloth) and seal tightly.
Take some clay or mud, or make a dirt-and-water mud pie; lay the fish over a burlap or gunny sack, and slap the mud right over the foil; pat on to cover both sides.
Wrap the burlap around, and tie with cord or string. Lift fish onto coals in pit; and lay something over it; a piece of sheet iron, some burlap, or any such thing you might have. Fill pit with dirt, and leave fish for a minimum of 6 hours.

After 6 hours or so, carefully dig out the fish. To serve, split at rib line, and fold meat aside. The backbone can be lifted right off.

BAKED WHOLE FISH

Make a small slit just below the gills. Pull out the liver and intestines, and wrap fish in foil. Bake in a slow oven, or buried in hot ashes under a campfire, about an hour per pound of fish.

FISH BAKED IN CLAY

Cover fish with a good thick coat of mud or clay. Bury under the ashes of a hot fire, and bake until the clay has hardened. When the casing is broken the scales will come right off.

CURED SMOKED FISH

Fillet the fish; if necessary, cut fillets again so that they are no thicker than 1 inch.
Soak fillets overnight in a brine:
> 2 cups salt
> 2 cups brown sugar
> 2 quarts water

Stir until salt and sugar are dissolved.
In the morning take the fish out of the brine and rinse in clear water. Spread fish out to air-dry for about 1 hour.
Place fish in smoker (see below) and smoke for 8-10 hours, depending on the degree of dryness that you like, and upon the thickness of the fish. Take the thinner pieces out before the thicker pieces.
If the fish is to be kept moist, wrap in foil. To preserve it you will have to freeze it. Under refrigeration it will keep for approximately 2 weeks. If the fish is smoked very dry, it may be kept without refrigeration.

To make a smoker:
For traveling, a collapsible wooden box may be made; old refrigerator racks may be set inside, and a hole cut in the top to let the smoke out.

To smoke fish:
Cut red willow; put into hibachi or into any old metal can with a vent hole cut in it. Sprinkle water over flames if necessary to keep them down; keep feeding the smoker with the willow, being careful at all times not to let it burst into flames.

COOKING FROZEN FISH

Thaw fish before cooking, preferably; if the fish is still frozen, double the cooking time.

BARBECUED FISH

Take a 6-pound chunk of fish, fresh salmon preferably, and clean it thoroughly.

Give the inside a shaking of salt and pepper; put in 3 generous slices of onion; break half a bay leaf into small bits and scatter it over the onion. Stick 1 whole allspice or 1 whole clove into the middle slice of onion.

Rub outside of fish with a little bacon fat or oil.

Wrap fish in foil and place over glowing coals. Cover with an old metal washpan or similar container. This gives you a domed barbecue which holds in the heat, and is good for baking potatoes.

Cook fish for ½ hour; turn and cook for another ½ hour.

FISH HEAD CHOWDER

Fish heads, preferably from
   large-headed fish such as trout
   or salmon
onions, chopped
green pepper, chopped (optional)
celery, chopped
garlic
butter
1 potato, cut into small chunks
stewed tomatoes, about 1 cup
1 bay leaf

Boil fish heads in water to cover until meat is tender; skim fat off top; strain liquid and reserve meat from cheeks.

Sauté onions, green pepper, celery and garlic in butter until semi-transparent; add to the liquid. Add tomatoes, potato and bay leaf; simmer until potato is tender. Season broth to taste, add fish meat, and serve.

BOILED TROUT (Bleu)

The fish should be fresh caught.

For each fish, boil 1 quart water, and add 2 tablespoons vinegar (or 3 tablespoons lemon juice) per fish.

Split and clean fish as quickly as possible, being careful not to rub off the natural coating on the skin. Plunge fish into the boiling water, and bring water to a boil again. Remove the pot from the heat and put a cover on it. Let this sit about 5 minutes for an 11-inch trout and 8 minutes for a 15-inch trout. If you follow these directions, the fish will turn a brilliant blue; should you not desire a blue fish, omit vinegar or lemon juice.

BAKED WHOLE TROUT

(For fish 3 pounds and up)
Open fish just enough to clean it. Fill cavity with a stalk of celery, a slice or two of onion, and seasoning to taste. Add a little mustard if desired.

Wrap fish securely with tin foil, and bake in a moderate oven about 35 minutes to a pound.

LAKE TROUT FILLETS

Skin and bone as many trout as required; cut into serving pieces.

Dip fillets into beaten egg, then into bread or cracker crumbs seasoned with salt and pepper.

Put cooking oil, butter or margarine into heavy skillet (iron is best) and fry until nicely browned.

While fish is cooking, heat 1 can (8 ounces or more, depending on the amount of fish used) tomato sauce; add 1 heaping tablespoon butter and seasoning to taste.

Pour tomato sauce over fillets and serve on heated platter.

BARBECUED WHOLE FISH

Push a stick into the fish next to the backbone; the stick should be on the side which is away from the fire, otherwise the fish will fall apart. When the first side is cooked, turn, and cook other side until fish is done.

FISH MULLIGAN

Cut carrots, potatoes and turnips into small pieces, and slice onion; boil in water for about 5 minutes.

Cut fish into chunks a couple of inches square; add this to the vegetables, along with 1 small bay leaf. Cook slowly until well done.

QUICK STEAMED FISH

Build a fire and let it burn down to red-hot coals.

Clean fish, cut in half, and cook in boiling water about 10 minutes. Remove fish, dry it a little, and sprinkle with seasoning to taste.

Rub the bottom of a roasting pan with a small amount of fat. Lay the fish over the rack in the pan; if you haven't a rack, place 3 or 4 small pieces of wood in the pan and lay the fish over this.

Cover pan, and place directly on hot coals for 5 minutes.

BAKED FISH WITH SAGE DRESSING

Clean fish and bone the ribs and backbone. Do not cut through the skin at the back.
Combine:
  1½ cups bread crumbs
  1 medium onion, finely chopped
  1 tablespoon raisins
  1 teaspoon sage
  salt and pepper to taste
  2 sprigs celery, finely chopped
  1 tablespoon butter
Stuff cavity of fish with this, and tie or roll in tin foil. Bake in a 375 F oven until done.

STEAMED FISH

Wipe fish with a damp cloth, and sprinkle with a little chopped celery and onion, about 1½ teaspoons per pound.

Wrap in dampened parchment paper and tie securely. Place in rapidly boiling water and boil about 10 minutes per inch of thickness for fresh fish, and about 20 minutes per inch of thickness for frozen fish.

BAKED FISH WITH LEMON-BUTTER SAUCE

Preheat oven to 350 F.

Cut fish into 2-pound chunks, and put into an ovenproof dish; add a few tablespoons water, or white wine if you wish. Cover, and bake about 25 minutes.
Melt:
  3 tablespoons butter
Add:
  2 teaspoons lemon juice
  1-2 teaspoons parsley, minced
  1 teaspoon chives, chopped
  2 tablespoons capers (optional)
Pour this over the fish, and serve.

BAKED FISH STEAKS

Sprinkle fish steaks with seasoning to taste, and let fish sit for a while. Preheat oven to 325 F.

Bake fish 20-30 minutes (depending on thickness of steaks) or until fish flakes easily with fork.

STEAMED FISH STEAKS

Place fish steaks on sheets of aluminum foil, and pour over them equal amounts of melted butter and white wine. Sprinkle with fresh minced herbs; parsley, chives, tarragon or basil are good. If dried herbs are used, a small pinch will do.

Wrap foil around fish so that it's sealed tightly; bake in moderately hot oven for 25-30 minutes.

BAKED STUFFED FISH

1-, 2- or 3-pound fish, or several
    smaller fish, with heads, tails
    and fins on
2 tablespoons butter
¼-½ cup onion, chopped
¼-½ cup celery, chopped
½ cup fresh mushrooms, sliced
    or diced (optional)
2 cups soft bread crumbs
½ teaspoon salt
pinch of marjoram
2 tablespoons butter,
    combined with
2 tablespoons lemon juice

Melt butter and sauté onion, celery
and mushrooms over a slow fire for 5
minutes; add bread, salt and marjoram,
and stuff into fish loosely.

Place fish in a baking dish and brush
with lemon juice-butter mixture. Bake
in a preheated 325 F oven for 20 minutes if the fish is 1 inch thick, 30
minutes for a fish that is 2 inches
thick, and so on. This is the approxi-
mate time for a fish which is of room
temperature; a cold fish will need a
slightly longer baking time.

Dressing variation:
Omit the mushrooms, and add ½-1 cup
whole, seedless green grapes, or 2 or 3
diced apples. Sage may be used in
place of marjoram.

ARCTIC FISH SALAD MOLD

1 envelope gelatin
½ cup cold water
¼ cup mayonnaise
1 pound cooked, flaked fish,
    any kind
1¼ cups celery, very finely
    chopped
1 tablespoon lemon juice
1 tablespoon capers
onion, finely chopped, to taste
tomato, chopped
relish (optional)

Sprinkle the gelatin over the water and
heat slowly to dissolve. Cool to room
temperature.

Fold gelatin into the mayonnaise
and combine with remaining ingredients. Pour into a mold, chill.

FISH SALAD SANDWICH FILLING

1 cup cooked fish
½-1 cup diced celery
    or cucumber
mayonnaise or French dressing
1 tablespoon parsley, chopped
onion, chopped, to taste
relish or chili sauce (optional)
tomato, chopped (optional)

Combine ingredients and serve on lettuce, or use as a sandwich filling.

FISH CHOWDER

Cut fish into 1½- to 2-inch chunks and
put into pot with water to cover.

Add ½ bay leaf, 1 or 2 allspice
berries, 1 sliced onion, diced celery
and small chunks of potato. Bring to a
slow boil, and simmer for about 25
minutes, until the vegetables are tender
and the fish is done. Add a little fresh
milk and a dab of butter the last few
minutes; salt to taste.

SALMON SALAD

1 cup cooked red salmon,
    fresh or canned
2½ cups cooked macaroni, shell
    or elbow style, chilled
1 cup celery, diced
2 or 3 tablespoons onion,
    chopped
1 cup peas, fresh or frozen,
    cooked
½ cup mayonnaise
½ teaspoon vinegar

Whip vinegar into the mayonnaise, and
combine with remaining ingredients.

FISH SALAD

Combine leftover cooked fish with
chopped celery hearts, mayonnaise
(enough to moisten) and a dash of
lemon juice. Chopped fresh chives may
be added, if desired.

FISH APPETIZER

½ pound fillet of whitefish,
   grayling or trout
½ teaspoon salt
2 tablespoons lemon juice
   or tarragon vinegar
2 or more tablespoons capers
white pepper, freshly ground
dash of celery salt
dash of cayenne
½ cup chili sauce
1 teaspoon dill weed (optional)
1 tablespoon fresh horseradish
onion, chopped, to taste

Steam fish and break into flaky pieces.
Combine ingredients, and taste for
seasoning. Chill before serving.

Variation:
Omit capers and season with fresh
minced dill; or add 1 tablespoon or
more chopped onion or chives, or
chopped celery.

BAKED TROUT or SALMON

Fill inside of fish with 1 can of tomatoes, salt, pepper, chopped celery,
chopped onion and Worcestershire
sauce. Cover fish with the same; bake
in a pan with the lid on, about 20-25
minutes for every 2 pounds of fish,
using a moderate oven.

BAKED TROUT WITH
SOUR CREAM

2 pounds lake trout fillets
¼ cup butter
1 tablespoon flour
½ cup sour cream
1 teaspoon salt
1/8 teaspoon pepper
1 5-ounce can mushrooms,
   chopped
½ cup tomatoes, chopped

Place fish on greased baking dish.
   Rub together the flour and butter
in a saucepan over low heat; blend in
sour cream, salt, pepper, mushrooms
and tomato. Pour over fish and bake
uncovered at 350 F for 25 minutes.
(Makes 4-6 servings.)

BROILED FISH WITH
GINGER MARINADE

Marinate fish fillets or steaks for several hours in a mixture of:
   ½ teaspoon ginger
   2 tablespoons soy sauce
   2 tablespoons lemon juice
   2 tablespoons oil
   2 scallions, cut into ½-inch
      pieces
Broil or barbecue about 6 inches from
flame.

Variations:
Add any of the following:
1 or 2 tablespoons dry sherry; 1 or 2
cloves garlic, crushed; 1 onion, sliced;
or 2 teaspoons dark brown sugar.

TROUT AURORA BOREALIS

Sprinkle salt all over the skin of the
fish on both sides, as much as you'd
normally use for seasoning.
   Let salt settle into the skin for 20
minutes; then broil, and the skin will
take on iridescent rainbow colors as
it cooks.

KING SALMON A LA DAWSON

Roll salmon steaks in flour.
   Butter a baking pan, and lay in
steaks. Cover with sliced onion, a little
salt, red and black pepper and ginger.
Pour over ½ can of tomatoes and
place bits of butter on top.
   Bake in a moderate oven for ½ hour.

BROILED FILLET OF GRAYLING

To achieve a brown color without over-
cooking the fish, sprinkle with paprika
before broiling.
   Broil fish about 5 inches away
from heat 5-10 minutes, or until fish
flakes easily with fork and begins to
exude milky fluid.

FREEZING OF
KLONDIKE GRAYLING

A simple and economical way to preserve fish.

Wash fish, and remove heads and tails. Put 2 or 3 fish each into clean milk cartons, and fill cartons with ice cold water to cover fish. Fold down tops and seal with masking tape. Place in freezer at once.

Thaw fish in sink or in a pan, at room temperature.

THAWING
FROZEN LAKE LABARGE TROUT
(Method Used in 1898)

Place fish before hot stove for 5 minutes, turning often. Insert butcher's knife around the head under the skin; take hold of skin and pull downwards, and fish will skin like a rabbit, though frozen hard.

Section 2

**BAKERY
BEANS
and
GARDEN VEGETABLES**

SOURDOUGH

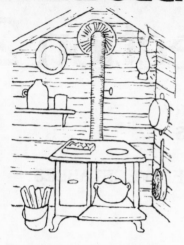

SOURDOUGH STARTER

Sourdough is a mixture of flour and water, fermented in various ways with natural yeast. Having a well-used starter guarantees that these organisms will be plentiful, but in lieu of the starter, a mixture of yeast, flour and warm water or potato water can be used. Oldtimers who had no yeast to begin with mixed flour, water and sugar and set it aside to ferment.

The starter is set by adding flour and water to it, and letting it sit in a warm place overnight. One cup of this starter is removed before other ingredients are added. This 1 cup of starter is the basis of future hotcakes, waffles and bread.

The more the starter is used, the better it will be. If it is not used once a week it may get a little too sour; when this happens just throw out some of it, and replace with the same amount of flour and water.

The starter should be kept in a cold place, but it should never be allowed to freeze. Nor should it be stored in a metal container; a wooden bowl or container is best. Oldtimers often used wooden buckets or hollowed-out logs as their sourdough pots.

To make your starter:

Get a cup of sourdough batter from a friend or neighbor, and mix it with 1 cup flour and 1 cup warm water (no hotter than 90 F). Let this stand in a warm place for about 12 hours, or until bubbles begin to form and it takes on a pleasantly sour aroma.

If you can't get a starter, take ½ ounce of yeast cake or packaged yeast, and combine with 2 cups flour and 2 cups warm water or potato water. Let mixture sit in a warm place for 24-36 hours.

SOURDOUGH BANNOCK

½ cup starter
1 cup warm water (no hotter than 90 F)
2½ cups unsifted wheat flour, or 2 cups wheat flour and ½ cup graham flour, corn flour or other flour
¾ teaspoon salt
1 teaspoon baking powder
½ teaspoon soda

Mix starter, water and 1 cup of the flour in a large bowl, at least 8 hours before baking time. Cover bowl, and keep at room temperature for 8 or more hours, depending on the degree of sourness desired.

Spread 1 cup of flour on bread board; turn dough out onto it.

Combine salt, baking powder, soda and the remaining ½ cup of flour, and sift over the top of the dough; mix into dough with hands, kneading lightly.

Roll out dough to ½ inch thickness, and cut with a round cutter. Place rounds in a greased, 9-inch square pan close together; let them rise for about ½ hour, then bake in a preheated, 375 F oven 30-35 minutes.

WHOLE WHEAT SOURDOUGH BREAD

(Slightly sour, very light and airy)

Mix together in a non-metal container:
    1 cup starter
    1½ cups warm water
    2 cups whole wheat flour*,
        freshly ground
Cover and set in a closed cupboard overnight.

Next morning remove ½ cup of the batter for use in future bakings, and store in a cool place.

Pour into a large bowl:
    2 cups warm water
    1½-2 teaspoons salt
    ¼ cup honey or maple syrup
        (optional)
Cover dough and set in a warm place for 30 minutes. Stir dough down, and add up to 4 cups whole wheat flour until the dough gets too stiff to stir. Knead about 100 times. Form loaves and sprinkle lightly with flour; place in pans and set in a warm place until dough is doubled in bulk. Bake at 400 F for 20 minutes, then turn heat down to 325 F and bake 20 minutes longer.

SOURDOUGH FRENCH BREAD
(Chewy)

    1½ cups water
    1 package yeast
    1 cup starter
    4 cups unsifted flour
    2 teaspoons salt
    2 teaspoons honey
    ½ teaspoon soda
    about 2 cups flour*, unsifted
Dissolve yeast in hot water. Pour into a large bowl; stir in the starter. Add the 4 cups of flour, salt, and syrup or honey. Stir vigorously 3 or 4 minutes.

Cover with towel and let rise 1½-2 hours (until doubled).

Mix soda with 1 cup of the remaining flour and stir into the dough.

Knead on floured board 5-10 minutes, adding from the remaining cup of flour if necessary; form oblong loaves.

Brush tops with water before baking, and slash diagonally with a razor blade.

Preheat oven to 400 F. Place a shallow pan in the bottom of the oven, and fill with ½ inch of boiling water. Bake loaves for 45 minutes, or until medium dark brown.

*2 cups of rye flour may be substituted for 2 cups wheat flour in the above recipes.

SOURDOUGH ENGLISH MUFFINS

    1 cup sourdough starter
    1 cake compressed yeast
    1 cup warm water (90 F)
    1 teaspoon salt
    3½ cups flour, unbleached,
        white, or whole wheat
    1 tablespoon melted butter
        (optional)
Crumble yeast into warm water in mixing bowl, and let it sit for 10 minutes. Add salt, starter and melted butter; beat in 2 cups flour gradually.

Let batter rise in a warm place (85 F) for 1½ hours or until it collapses back into the bowl.

Beat in remaining 1½ cups flour, and knead briefly, adding a little more flour if necessary. Form rounds ¾ inch thick and about 3 inches in diameter. Dip top and bottom in cornmeal if you wish. Let rounds rise for 10 minutes, then bake on a griddle until well browned; turn and brown the other side.

To serve, split muffins and toast them. Spread with butter or cream cheese, and raspberry jam or honey.

HOTCAKES

SOURDOUGH HOTCAKES

Make your basic batter the night before, mixing:
- ½ cup starter
- 2 cups warm water
- 2-2½ cups flour

Cover container (do not use metal) and let it set in a warm place overnight, or 10-12 hours. Save ½ cup of this batter for future bakings.
Add to the remaining batter:
- 1 teaspoon soda
- ½ teaspoon salt
- 1 tablespoon wild flower honey or 1 tablespoon maple syrup
- 2 eggs

Beat with fork. Stir in:
- 2 tablespoons oil, or melted butter (optional)
- a handful of wild blueberries* (optional)

Pour batter onto a hot griddle and brown cakes on both sides. Serve with blueberry syrup, rosehip jam or honey.

*Only wild blueberries should be used; the commercial variety will be too mushy in pancakes.

SOURDOUGH BUCKWHEAT CAKES

Use recipe above, but replace ¼-½ cup wheat flour with ¼-½ cup buckwheat flour, and add 1 tablespoon dark molasses.

OLD TIME OATMEAL PANCAKES

- ½ cup flour
- 1 teaspoon baking powder
- ½ teaspoon salt
- 1 egg
- 1½ cups cooked oatmeal
- ¾ cup milk, either fresh, evaporated, or dried reconstituted
- 2 tablespoons melted butter

Sift together dry ingredients; beat in egg, and stir in remaining ingredients. Bake on a hot griddle.

QUICK BUCKWHEAT CAKES

- 1 pint buckwheat flour
- 2 heaping teaspoons baking powder
- 1 teaspoon salt
- 1 tablespoon brown sugar
- 1 pint cold water

Thoroughly mix baking powder, sugar and salt with flour. When ready to bake, add water and stir. Bake immediately.

FILL-ME-UP PANCAKES

- ½ cup whole wheat flour
- 1 cup white unbleached flour
- ½ cup rice polishing, barley flour or wheat germ, corn flour, etc.
- (Vary the proportions, to taste, using 2 cups of flour altogether.)
- 2-3 teaspoons baking powder
- ½ teaspoon sea salt
- ¼ cup brown sugar
- 1½-2 cups buttermilk or yogurt
- 4 eggs
- ½ cup safflower oil

Mix dry ingredients; add slowly to buttermilk or yogurt; stir in oil and eggs.
  Bake in a moderately hot pan or on a griddle. Serve with pure maple syrup or honey, and a dollop of yogurt.

BANNOCK

Add wild berries, approximately ¼ cup. Raisins may be used in place of berries; also cinnamon, or anything you have that tastes good.

OLD COUNTRY BANNOCK
(The original Scottish Bannock)

1 cup wheat flour and
1 cup barley flour
   or 1 cup wheat flour and
   1 cup flour or oatmeal
½ teaspoon salt
3-4 teaspoons baking powder
2-3 tablespoons brown sugar
   (optional)
2 tablespoons cold butter
3/4 - 7/8 cup water

Mix dry ingredients well. Cut in butter with forks, breaking into fine particles. Add water slowly, enough to make a soft dough. Dust hands with flour and knead dough (this is optional).

Bake in a greased skillet next to the hot coals of a fire and brown on both sides, taking care not to burn.

CAMPFIRE BANNOCK

2 cups flour
½ teaspoon salt
2 teaspoons baking powder
2 tablespoons tallow (lard),
   finely chopped
enough water to make a soft
   dough

Heat frying pan over hot coals; add enough lard to cover bottom of pan.

Spoon dough into pan; flatten top, and fry until bannock is well raised. Turn and cook the other side; add more lard if needed. Do not have frying pan too hot. You can also cook this as a dumpling in a stew.

GOLD NUGGET BANNOCK

"Little golden nuggets" (of wheat germ) tenderize the bannock and give it a nut-like flavor; only fresh wheat germ should be used.

a scant 2 cups flour
½ teaspoon salt
2½ teaspoons baking powder
   (double-acting)
2-6 tablespoons fresh wheat germ
a scant cup water

Mix flour, baking powder, salt and wheat germ thoroughly.

Pour in water, enough to make a sticky dough, and stir quickly for just half a minute.

Drop by spoonfuls into a greased pan or dutch oven, and bake or broil in a hot oven (450 F) for 12-15 minutes. Brush with butter while still hot, and serve with honey or jam.

BERRY BANNOCK

Prepare bannock dough, but do not use any fat in the recipe, and for half of the baking powder substitute 1 teaspoon cream of tartar.

BREAD

BASIC YEAST BREAD

¼ cup warm water
1 ounce yeast
1/8 teaspoon ginger (optional)
Dissolve yeast in water with ginger.
Add:
    1-2 teaspoons salt
    1 cup warm water and
    1/8-1/4 cup clover honey
      or wild flower honey
    2 cups flour, white, unbleached,
      or whole wheat
Beat until smooth.
Stir in:
    6 tablespoons milk
    1½ cups warm water
    1/8-1/4 cup soft butter or oil
Beat into the batter, one cup at a
time, until smooth and elastic:
    3 cups flour
Measure:
    1 cup flour
Sprinkle about half of it onto a board,
and knead 5-10 minutes, adding more
flour as needed.

Put dough into a greased bowl and
turn it over, so that it's greased on all
sides. Let it rise in a warm place for
1-1½ hours, until almost doubled in
bulk.

Punch dough down, and shape into
loaves; place in bread pans and raise in
a warm place for 45 minutes.

Bake in a preheated, 375 F oven
about 45 minutes. Brush bread with
butter while still warm, if a soft crust
is desired.

Yeast Bread Variations

SPROUTS BREAD

Prepare basic yeast bread dough, using
whole wheat flour. After the first
rising, punch it down, and add a cup of
finely chopped fresh bean sprouts.

Shape loaves and allow to rise in
pans for 45 minutes; bake.

MIXED GRAIN BREAD

Omit 2 cups of wheat flour, and substitute 2 cups oat flour, rice flour,
millet flour, soy flour, rye flour, or
barley flour.

Heavier grains such as wheat grits,
buckwheat flour or wheat germ should
be used in smaller quantities: ½-1 cup
in place of the same amount of wheat
flour.

HAMBURGER BUNS

After the first rising, punch down the
dough and form smooth-topped balls
about 2 inches in diameter. Place in
pan, pressing to flatten. Let dough rise
until almost doubled, about 30 minutes. Brush with a mixture of beaten
egg white and water, for a glazed
crust; sprinkle with dried onion flakes
(which have been soaked in a little
water until soft) or with sesame seeds
or poppy seeds, if desired. Bake in a
375 F oven 12-15 minutes.

CRACKER BREAD

Make a yeast bread dough, and let it
rise once, for 45 minutes.

Shape dough into 2-inch balls. Roll
out into rounds about ¼ inch thick.
Sprinkle with sesame seeds or poppy
seeds and roll again to press them in.

Preheat oven to 400 F.

Bake rounds on the lowest rack of
the oven, a few at a time, for about 3
minutes, or until lightly browned. Turn
and bake another 3 minutes.

RYE HARDTACK

1 package dry yeast
2 cups warm water
1 teaspoon salt
4½-5 cups rye flour

Dissolve the yeast in the water. Add the salt and gradually beat in 4 cups flour. The dough should be soft. Cover lightly and let rise in the mixing bowl in a warm place until doubled in bulk (about 1 hour).

Sprinkle a board generously with flour and turn the dough out onto it. Shape into a smooth ball and divide into 4 parts. Form each into a round ball, using flour freely to keep the dough from sticking, but be careful not to work the extra flour into the dough. Roll out carefully, powdering any sticky spot with flour, until the dough is about ¼-½ inch thick. Keep the shape round.

Using a large spatula, remove the round to a baking sheet that has been greased and floured. Prick the round all over with a fork; cut a hole in the center (using a round cutter about 2 inches in diameter) and let rise in a warm place for 15 minutes.

Bake in a very hot oven (450 F) for 10-15 minutes or until the bread feels firm when touched. The rounds should still bend when they are removed from the oven. Cool on a rack.

Let the bread dry until it is properly crisp. It can be dried in a cool oven (220 F) for 6-8 hours, or it can be hung from poles, and slowly dried in a warm, dry place.

SOFT CORN BREAD

2 cups well-cooked cornmeal
2 cups well-cooked rice, flaky*
¼ cup flour
2 cups milk
2 teaspoons baking powder
3 eggs

Mix ingredients, separating the yolks and whites of eggs.

Bake in hot oven, using a flat pan, for 20 minutes. Cut with pie knife. Serve with butter, honey or maple syrup.

*For flaky, golden-colored rice:
Bring 2 cups of water to a boil. Add 1 cup brown rice, ½ teaspoon salt and ¼ teaspoon turmeric, and heat until boiling.

Set oven temperature at 325-350 F. Cover rice and put into oven to steam; after 15 minutes or so, turn the oven off and leave rice for 45 minutes to an hour, or slightly longer. Stir rice with a fork to fluff.

STEAMED BROWN BREAD

1 cup corn meal
1 cup rye flour
1 cup whole wheat or
    graham flour
1 teaspoon salt
1 teaspoon soda
½ cup molasses
2 cups buttermilk or water with
    ½ teaspoon cider vinegar added
1 cup raisins

Combine flours and salt in bowl; mix well.

Dissolve soda in 2 tablespoons hot water, and stir at once into the molasses. Combine with the buttermilk (or water) and pour into the dry ingredients. Lightly flour the raisins and mix in.

Drop the dough into 3 or 4 well-greased cans of medium size, filling them two-thirds full. Cover cans tightly with foil, and place them in a large pot with 1-2 inches of water on the bottom. Simmer gently for 2-3 hours, until cooked through.

Open bottom of can and push out bread to slice.

BEANS

BETTY TAYLOR'S BAKED BEANS

1 pound pinto beans
1 medium cooking onion
½ pound bacon or salt pork
salt
1 7-ounce tin tomato sauce
3 tablespoons molasses
1 chili pepper or
   2 dashes Tabasco
1 shake garlic salt
1 teaspoon dry mustard
pepper to taste

Wash beans well in colander; place beans in a saucepan with water and float out the poor beans.

Chop up onion; put beans, onion and salt in pot with enough water to cover. Cook until beans are soft.

Fry bacon; put grease and meat into the bean pot, along with the tomato sauce, spices and molasses.

Transfer the above into a stone bean crock, and bake at 300 F for 4 hours. Be sure that the beans are well covered with liquid at start of baking.

KLONDIKE BAKED BEANS

Soak ½ pound navy beans overnight in water to cover.

The next day put beans and water onto stove; add a bay leaf and about 2 teaspoons salt; simmer slowly for 2 hours.

Stir in ½ teaspoon dry mustard; ½ teaspoon chili powder; a dash of oregano; a light sprinkling of Worcestershire sauce; 3 tablespoons chili sauce; 1 chopped onion; 1 clove garlic, crushed; 1 small tin of tomato paste; 1 fresh tomato, chopped; and ¼ cup molasses.

Bake in a slow oven with the cover on for about 4-5 hours, or until tender; when the beans have cooked for 2-3 hours, taste for seasoning, and add more water if they seem dry.

BEAN SOUP

1 pound marrow beans, navy
   beans, or lima beans
3 quarts cold water
1 ham bone, or a piece of ham
6 celery stalks, finely chopped
½ onion, minced
1 clove garlic, crushed
1 carrot, diced
½ bay leaf
½ cup mountain sorrel, chopped
¼ cup parsley, minced
3 medium potatoes,
   cooked and mashed
1½ teaspoons salt, or to taste

Soak beans in cold water to cover overnight; drain.

Add the 3 quarts of cold water and the ham bone to the beans; simmer very slowly for 1-2 hours. The remaining ingredients are added during the last 30 minutes of cooking. Taste for seasoning.

BEAN SALAD

2 cups kidney beans
2 cups cut green beans
2 cups cut yellow beans
2 cups garbanzo beans (optional)
1 medium sized sweet onion,
   sliced
1 bell pepper, sliced
French dressing

Combine the beans, which have been pre-cooked or canned, with onion and bell pepper. Coat with French dressing to taste, and sprinkle with additional vinegar and brown sugar if desired.

SOUP

SOYBEAN SOUP

2 cups dried soybeans
1½ quarts water (for soaking)
1 ham bone
3 quarts water
1 cup onion, chopped
1 cup celery, chopped, with
    leaves
½ cup turnips, chopped
1 cup tomatoes, or tomato puree

Soak beans overnight; drain, and put into kettle.
    Add ham bone and water. Cover and simmer 3 hours.
    After 3 hours add onions, celery, turnips and tomato; cover and simmer for 1 hour.
    The soup may be pureed in the blender or pressed through a sieve if a smooth consistency is desired.
    Chill soup, and remove fat.
    Melt 2 tablespoons butter, and stir into 2 tablespoons flour. Heat soup and stir in mixture. (This thickening procedure is optional.)
    Bring soup to a boil and season with salt, pepper and ½ teaspoon paprika; stir; sprinkle with 2 table-spoons minced parsley. (Makes 3 quarts; serves 10-12.)

TOMATO SOUP

Stew a clove of garlic along with some minced parsley and a bit of minced basil or thyme in a little oil; add cut-up tomatoes, and sprinkle with whole meal flour. Cook over low heat for a little while, then add some vegetable-seasoned broth; it takes about ½ hour cooking. Puree soup in blender or through sieve; a little milk may be added, if desired. Sprinkle with chives and serve.

VEGETABLE BORSCH

1 bunch beets, diced
beet tops, cut into fine shreds
1 stalk celery, chopped
¼ cabbage
1 carrot, sliced
Simmer slowly in water to cover for 1 hour. Serve hot or cold with a dollop of sour cream or yogurt.

VEGETABLE SOUP

2-4 tablespoons pearl barley*
1½ quarts water

Simmer barley for 20 minutes.
Add:
    2-3 tablespoons mixed dried
        vegetable flakes (with onion
        and red bell pepper)
    1 carrot, sliced
    1 stalk celery, finely chopped
        (optional)
    about ¼ cup cabbage, finely
        shredded
    about ½ cup string beans, fresh
        or frozen, finely cut, or
        zucchini, diced

Cook gently until vegetables are tender, 15-20 minutes.
Add:
    1 can peas
    ½-1 can tomatoes, stewed
        tomatoes, tomato sauce or
        tomato juice; or mixed
        vegetable juice, to taste
Season with vegetable seasoning powder, onion powder and soy sauce or salt.

*Rice may be used in place of barley.

SALAD

HORS D'OEUVRE SALAD

Take an assortment of vegetables, cut them up, and arrange them attractively on a large serving platter:

celery sticks
carrot sticks
rutabaga sticks
cucumber wedges
bell pepper slices
romaine lettuce, the
    smaller leaves
cherry tomatoes or
    tomato wedges
radishes

Serve with mayonnaise or avocado dip.

TOSSED SALAD DELUXE

Rub salad bowl with a little chopped onion and garlic; toss in lettuce, which has been torn into bite-sized pieces, 1 or 2 tablespoons minced parsley, then celery, chopped fine, and radishes and cucumbers sliced very thin.

Root vegetables such as beet, carrot and turnip should be finely grated, and added in small quantities. Beets are especially good (1 small beet to a head of lettuce) because they're sweet, and they give your salad color.

Toss salad with oil—preferably cold-pressed salad oil—and vinegar or lemon juice (about 1 tablespoon oil and 1 teaspoon vinegar or lemon juice to a head of lettuce). Toss 30 times.

Tomatoes, if used, are best laid over the salad and tossed in just before serving; otherwise they will "weep."

Sprinkle salad lightly with vegetable seasoning salt or salt, and add a pinch of tarragon or basil if desired.

Cheese (grated or diced), meat or fowl (cut in shoestring strips), or small cubes of fish may be added; serve with additional dressing.

COLESLAW

½ head cabbage
¼-½ cup mayonnaise
1-2 teaspoons honey
¼ teaspoon salt
1 teaspoon lemon juice (optional)
paprika

Cut cabbage into shreds.

Stir the honey, salt, and lemon juice into the mayonnaise, blending well; mix into the cabbage.

Variations:
Season with ½ teaspoon dill seed or celery seed.

Add shredded carrot or minced parsley.

Mix mayonnaise with yogurt, half and half.

CARROTSLAW

Scrub or peel carrots, and grate finely. Toss with mayonnaise to taste. Grated onion may be added if desired.

CUCUMBER SALAD

1 cucumber
vinegar
soy sauce
salad oil

Peel the cucumber if you think that it might be waxed. If it's not waxed, score it lengthways with a fork and slice it into paper-thin slices with a sharp knife.

Sprinkle with soy sauce, oil and vinegar. Serve chilled.

TOMATO SALAD

6 ripe, firm tomatoes
¼-½ cup salad oil
lemon juice or vinegar
1 tablespoon basil, finely
   chopped
1 tablespoon chives, finely cut

Cut tomatoes into fairly thick slices and sprinkle with remaining ingredients.

WALNUT SALAD

3 crisp, sweet apples
1 tablespoon lemon juice
1 cup celery, sliced on the
   diagonal
¼ cup mayonnaise
¼ cup French salad dressing
¼ cup walnuts, chopped
large lettuce leaves

Peel apples, cut into quarters, core, and cut into thin slices; sprinkle with lemon juice. Toss apples and celery together; cover and chill.

Just before serving: add remaining ingredients; toss lightly and serve over lettuce.

SALAD DRESSING
WITH HERBS

1/3 cup oil
1/3 cup apple cider vinegar or
   lemon juice
1 teaspoon dried herbs
   (a mixture of dill weed, sage
   and marjoram or thyme, or
   others)

1 clove garlic (optional)

Mix ingredients, and set in the refrigerator to blend for several days before using.

MAYONNAISE

½-¾ cup salad oil
1 large egg yolk
2 teaspoons vinegar
2 teaspoons lemon juice
½ teaspoon salt
½ teaspoon vegetable
   seasoning (optional)

Have ingredients at room temperature.

Beat the egg yolk.

Pour in ¼ cup of the oil, beating all the time.

Add remaining oil drop by drop, beating constantly. If a blender is used, run it a few seconds after each addition. Blend in seasonings when the mayonnaise begins to thicken.

RUSSIAN DRESSING

This dressing is almost a salad in itself.

mayonnaise, or half yogurt
   and half mayonnaise
bell pepper, chopped
chives or onions
tomato, peeled and chopped,
   or tomato puree
parsley, chopped
lemon juice
celery, chopped very finely

Serve on tossed salad, lettuce wedges, or use as a sandwich spread.

GARDEN VEGETABLES

ASPARAGUS

Break off ends where they begin to lose their crisp texture. Steam 8-20 minutes with a minimum amount of water and covered with a close-fitting lid.

BEANS

Cook gently over a slow fire with a minimum amount of water and tightly covered, for 10-20 minutes.

BROCCOLI

Steam, preferably in an upright position, 15 minutes.

BRUSSELS SPROUTS

Steam in eough water to keep them from scorching, for 12-15 minutes.

CABBAGE

Cut cabbage into quarters, and cook, tightly covered, with a little water added to the pot, 15-20 minutes.

CARROTS

Scrub or peel carrots; cut into slices and steam in a small amount of boiling water, with the lid on, for 20-30 minutes, until tender.

CAULIFLOWER

Cook with a little water (and a dash of lemon juice, if desired, to keep it white) 10 minutes for 2-inch pieces, 15 minutes or longer for a whole cauliflower.

GREENS

Steam with a sprinkling of water for 4-6 minutes.

PEAS

Lay a large rinsed leaf of lettuce in the bottom of the pan; put peas on top of the lettuce and cook gently with the lid on, for 9-11 minutes.

POTATOES

Baking Potatoes:
Prick potatoes and bake in 425 F oven 20 minutes; turn heat down to 300 F and bake 20-40 minutes longer.

Small or Thin-skinned Potatoes:
Scrub potatoes, cut into pieces of desired size, and steam for 12-18 minutes, in enough water to keep them from burning.

SUMMER SQUASH

Slice or dice squash and cook in a small quantity of water with a tight-fitting lid about 25 minutes.

WINTER SQUASH

Cut squash in half; rub with oil or butter and bake in a 325 F oven 1-1½ hours, or in a 400 F oven for 50 minutes.

SAVORIES

BEET AND CABBAGE RELISH

4 cups raw cabbage, finely
   shredded
4 cups cooked beets, chopped
2 cups brown sugar
½ cup vinegar
¼ cup water
1 tablespoon horseradish
Seal in sterilized jars.

PIMIENTO-ONION RELISH

2/3 cup water
1/3 cup cider vinegar
1/2 teaspoon minced herbs*
2 tablespoons honey
1 4-ounce jar whole pimientos,
   quartered
a medium onion, thinly sliced
Pour into sterilized jars; seal.

*Parsley, chives, tarragon and/or chervil.

CHILI SAUCE

2 cans (28 ounces) tomatoes
1 bell pepper, diced (optional)
½ cup onion, finely chopped
1 cup apple, finely chopped
1½ cups celery, finely chopped
1 cup vinegar
¾-1 cup sugar, brown or white
2 teaspoons salt
1 teaspoon cinnamon
1/8 teaspoon cayenne pepper
12 cloves
6 whole allspice berries
   (ground allspice can be used)
Tie cloves and allspice into a bag, and
combine the bag and all the ingredients
in a large kettle. Bring to the boiling
point and simmer until thickened.
Remove spice bag and pour chili sauce
into sterilized jars; seal, and store in a
cool, dark place.

HOT SLAW

½ cabbage, shredded
2 egg yolks, slightly beaten
¾ cup cold water
1 teaspoon butter
¼ cup hot vinegar
½ teaspoon salt
pineapple, diced (optional)
Mix egg yolks, cold water, vinegar and
salt. Cook over hot water, stirring
constantly until thickened.
   Add cabbage and some diced pineapple (if desired) and serve when
heated.

SAUERKRAUT

cabbage, shredded
juniper berries
mustard seeds
coriander seeds (optional)
salt, ½ ounce per cabbage
onions, sliced (optional)
marjoram, thyme or favorite
   herb, a pinch (optional)
Place a layer of cabbage 1 inch deep
in a clean crock or container. Scatter
juniper berries, mustard seeds and
coriander seeds over this—if you aren't
using the coriander seeds, double the
quantity of mustard seeds. Add a small
pinch of salt.
   Lay onions (optional) over cabbage in a layer ½ inch thick. Cover
with another layer of cabbage and
seasoning, etc., until the container
is full.
   Press down tightly; cover and place
a weight on top. Allow to ferment.
The whole process should be done in a
warm room. The container should be
kept in a room that is warmer than
68 F for the first 2 or 3 weeks; then it
should be kept in a cold place.

GARDENING INDOORS

GROWING HERBS INDOORS

Some herbs which can be grown inside are: parsley, chives, dill, chervil, savory, thyme, tarragon, rosemary and marjoram.

Prepare potting soil, mixing 1 part garden loam, 1 part coarse sand and 1 part rotted compost.* Add 1 pint of bone meal to each bushel of mix.

Take earthenware pots which are at least 4 inches in diameter, and fill to about an inch from the top.

Spread stones or broken pieces of earthenware over the bottom of a tray; the tray should be at least 2 or 3 inches deep. Place pots over tray. Plant seeds about as deep as they are wide.

Keep water in the tray at all times, but not so high that it touches the pot. Water frequently from the top. Once every 10 days, immerse the pot in water for an hour.

*Compost:
2 or 3 inches of peelings, leaves, garden residue, sawdust, etc., a sprinkling of lime, then a 5- to 7-inch layer of dirt. Repeat 2 or 4 times at least. The more layers you have the better it is. (You'll get more complete microbial action in less time, and without having to turn the compost, if the pile is raised a foot above the ground.)

SPROUTS

Fresh sprouts can be grown indoors during the winter, without soil; they are a good source of enzymes, the B vitamins, vitamin C and minerals.

Any seed which hasn't been chemically treated can be sprouted.

sunflower seeds (eat before
    longer than ¼ inch)
radish seeds
whole cereal berries, such as
    wheat, barley, oats and rye
watercress seeds
alfalfa seeds
mung beans (Chinese beans)
soy beans

Take a large glass jar which is scrupulously clean. Put seeds into jar and cover with water. Soak 2 hours for small seeds such as alfalfa, and 8 hours for large seeds such as soy beans.

Drain off the water, using a saucer to keep the seeds from falling out. Rinse with water and drain again.

Leave the jar lying on its side, and repeat the draining and rinsing process once or twice daily for 4-6 days. Leave in a dark place the first few days, then put the jar onto the window sill so as to get some sun on the sprouts. After 4 days, they are usually mature enough to eat.

To serve, wash sprouts, removing outer skin of the original seed.

The larger sprouts, such as bean sprouts, are often stir-steam cooked, as for Chinese Chop Suey; or chopped, and baked in bread. They may be sprouted in clean sand in a flower pot; they have to soak for 8 hours first. The smaller seed sprouts are best done in the jar, and can be eaten in salads, in sandwiches and in soup.

Section 3

EDIBLE
WILD PLANTS

MUSHROOMS

and

BERRIES

EDIBLE WILD PLANTS

FIREWEED SPINACH

Pick fireweed before it goes to bud, or when it is 2-6 inches high.

Steam it in a pot with the lid on, over a few drops of water. Cook like spinach, testing with a fork to see that it's done.

Sprinkle with butter or oil, and lemon juice or vinegar; salt to taste.

POTPOURRI TEA

A colorful tea made from northern wild plants.

> fireweed leaves
> rose hips and seeds
> rose petals
> strawberry leaves
> raspberry leaves
> blue violets
> bearberry leaves
> sage

Gather together plants of your choice. Dry them; then grind or pulverize. To make tea, pour boiling water over and steep for 15 minutes.

FIREWEED
(Epilobium angustifolium)

The floral emblem of the Yukon grows 2-7 feet high; the flowers vary in color from white, which is rare, to magenta; the brilliant petals glow translucently in the Yukon's long summer sunshine. This is a hardy late-blooming flower which stays on long after the other Yukon wildflowers are gone.

The plants should be picked in the shoot stage, or when they are less than half a foot high. They can be eaten raw, chopped up and added to salad, or they can be cooked as greens. The leaves are rich in vitamins C and A.

DWARF FIREWEED
(Epilobium latifolium)

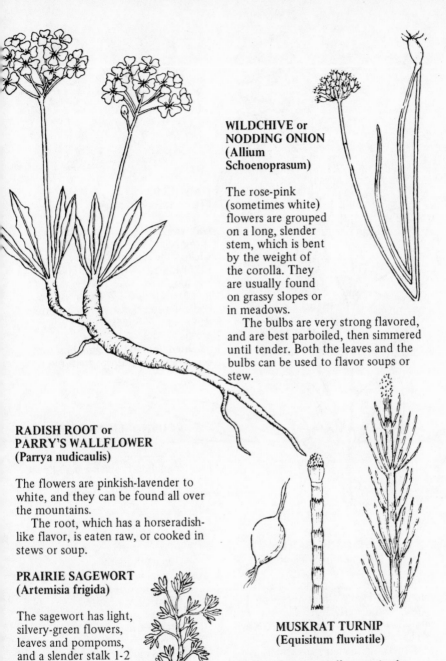

WILDCHIVE or NODDING ONION (Allium Schoenoprasum)

The rose-pink (sometimes white) flowers are grouped on a long, slender stem, which is bent by the weight of the corolla. They are usually found on grassy slopes or in meadows.

    The bulbs are very strong flavored, and are best parboiled, then simmered until tender. Both the leaves and the bulbs can be used to flavor soups or stew.

RADISH ROOT or PARRY'S WALLFLOWER (Parrya nudicaulis)

The flowers are pinkish-lavender to white, and they can be found all over the mountains.

    The root, which has a horseradish-like flavor, is eaten raw, or cooked in stews or soup.

PRAIRIE SAGEWORT (Artemisia frigida)

The sagewort has light, silvery-green flowers, leaves and pompoms, and a slender stalk 1-2 feet high. It grows in dry, open areas.

    Dried and crushed, it is a popular seasoning used most often in dressings for domestic or wild fowl, and for fish and game recipes.

MUSKRAT TURNIP (Equisitum fluviatile)

The "muskrat turnip" grows in the shallow water of lakes and marshes.

    The small root is the part that is eaten by small water animals and humans. It is sweet and best when eaten raw.

43

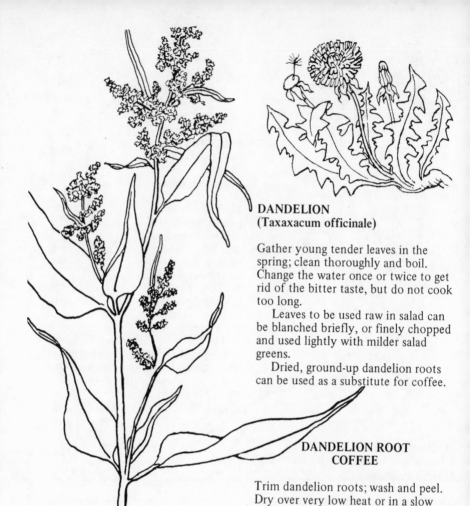

DANDELION
(Taxaxacum officinale)

Gather young tender leaves in the spring; clean thoroughly and boil. Change the water once or twice to get rid of the bitter taste, but do not cook too long.

Leaves to be used raw in salad can be blanched briefly, or finely chopped and used lightly with milder salad greens.

Dried, ground-up dandelion roots can be used as a substitute for coffee.

DANDELION ROOT COFFEE

Trim dandelion roots; wash and peel. Dry over very low heat or in a slow oven; then grind, and use as you would coffee.

WILD RHUBARB
(Polygonum alaskanum)

Wild rhubarb grows in moist soil, often along river banks, and is best picked in late June and early July. The flowers are white, and the plant grows 2-6 feet high.

The tart, red stems are usually cut in chunks and stewed with a little water. Rhubarb takes well to honey as a sweetening, especially if the honey is unprocessed and has a natural "tang."

(Rhubarb drawing, courtesy of A.E. Porsild)

RHUBARB RELISH

1 quart rhubarb
1 quart onions, finely chopped
3 cups brown sugar
1 pint cider vinegar
1 teaspoon salt
1 teaspoon cinnamon
1 teaspoon each allspice
    and cloves (optional)
red pepper (optional)

Cook to desired consistency* and seal in sterilized jars.

*Some people prefer it raw, or just slightly cooked; others like it well boiled.

BEAR ROOT, ESKIMO POTATO or PEA VINE
(Hedysarum alpinum)

(Drawing courtesy of A.E. Porsild)

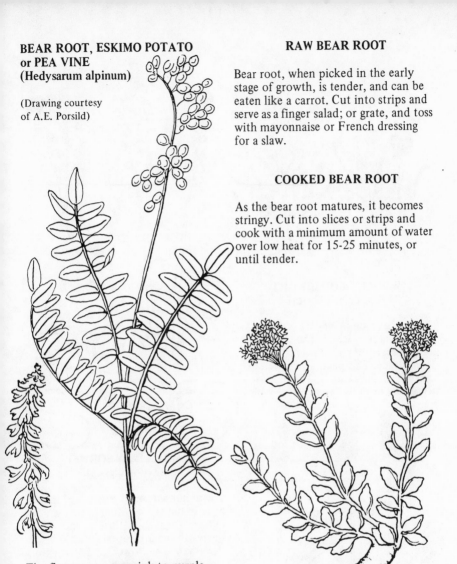

RAW BEAR ROOT

Bear root, when picked in the early stage of growth, is tender, and can be eaten like a carrot. Cut into strips and serve as a finger salad; or grate, and toss with mayonnaise or French dressing for a slaw.

COOKED BEAR ROOT

As the bear root matures, it becomes stringy. Cut into slices or strips and cook with a minimum amount of water over low heat for 15-25 minutes, or until tender.

The flowers are rose-pink to purple. The plant grows up to 2½ feet high, often in loose soil, near creek beds, on rocky slopes or in spruce forests; the leaves are a rich green.

The creamy colored tap root is 3-6 inches long. It is eaten raw or cooked.

Do not confuse the edible bear root with the *Hedysarum Mackenzii,* which is reported to be slightly poisonous.

The leaves and stems of the *Mackenzii* species are covered with fine hairs, most noticeable underneath the leaves, which are grayish green; and the plant is stouter.

ROSEROOT
(Sedum Rosea)

The flowers are purple or dark crimson, more rarely pink, and in some places, yellow. They are commonly found along creeks.

The root, and also the young shoots and leaves, may be eaten raw or boiled.

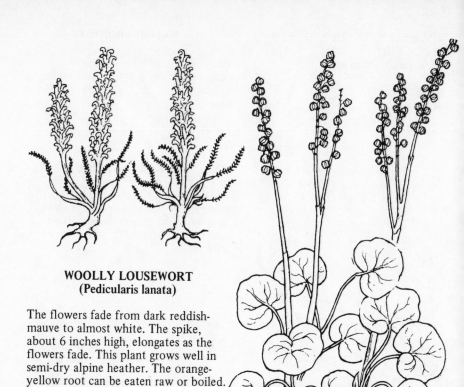

WOOLLY LOUSEWORT
(Pedicularis lanata)

The flowers fade from dark reddish-mauve to almost white. The spike, about 6 inches high, elongates as the flowers fade. This plant grows well in semi-dry alpine heather. The orange-yellow root can be eaten raw or boiled.

MOUNTAIN SORREL
(Oxyria digyna)

The mountain sorrel grows 4-24 inches high, in moist soil; often in rocky outcrops near snow flushes, and on the north side of slopes, where it is shadowed. The flowers and leaves are green, tinged with red.

Eat raw or cooked.

MOUNTAIN MEADOW BISTORT
(Polygonum bistorta)

The flowers are pink and white, and they grow 5-10 inches high. You can usually find them in bogs or meadows.

The root is rich in starch and lightly astringent; you may find it more palatable if soaked in water for several hours before cooking.

MARINATED SALAD WITH WILD GREENS

Make a tossed salad, using only ½ the lettuce which you plan for the salad. Add a few chopped leaves of fireweed, mountain sorrel or wintercress, in proportions to taste. Let this sit in the refrigerator for 2 hours or longer.

Just before serving time, toss in remaining lettuce.

46

BLACK SPRUCE
SPRUCE BUD TEA

Steep fresh tips of spruce in boiling water for 5 minutes or longer, and you will have a tea that is rich in Vitamin C.

WILLOW

The young shoots are rich in Vitamin C and can be cooked as greens, but they are decidedly sour.

WINTERCRESS or BITTERCRESS
(Barbarea orthoceras)

The plants grow from 1-2 feet high, all tangled together in creeks along the banks of streams and in moist places. The flowers are yellow.

The young leaves are eaten raw or boiled, in salad, sandwiches or soup.

LICHEN

Lichen is valuable as an emergency food, especially in the winter.

Most northern lichens contain a bitter acid which can be very irritating to the human stomach; it can be removed by soaking or boiling. Soak and drain several times, adding a teaspoon of soda to the water each time, to neutralize the acid.

Dry the lichen in the sun or in an oven, and pound it to a powder. Add the powder to soups or stews, make it into hot cereal, or use it as a substitute for half the flour in recipes for bread or bannock. It is very nutritious.

POPLAR

The sap layer, a soft tissue lying between the wood and outer bark, is very nourishing; it is scraped off and eaten raw, or cut into strips and cooked like noodles in soups or stews. Dried and powdered, it can be used as flour.

EDIBLE MUSHROOMS

STEAMED MUSHROOMS

Put the mushrooms into the top of a double boiler with a sprinkling of salt and a little water (about ½ cup water to 1 pound mushrooms).

Steam over boiling water for about 20 minutes, or until the mushrooms are tender. The broth may be used for stews, sauces and soups.

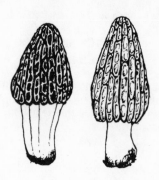

CONIC MOREL
(Morchella Conica [left] and Morchella Angusticeps [right])

The caps are ¾ inch-2 inches high, pointed, and dark brown in color, with long, blackish ribs. The flesh is watery, mild tasting and fine flavored. They come early in the year, and can be picked in May, June and July.

SAUTEED MUSHROOMS

Slice mushrooms; sauté in butter or oil or in a combination of oil and butter for 5-20 minutes. Add chopped onion, if desired. Salt lightly. During the last few minutes of cooking, a bit of crushed garlic or a sprinkling of minced parsley, paprika and/or dry white wine can be added, to taste.

MARINATED MUSHROOMS (UNCOOKED)

Cover sliced, raw mushrooms with oil and a little lemon juice, or with French dressing. Season to taste with minced herbs, onion and salt. Marinate in refrigerator overnight. Drain, and serve as hors d'oeuvres.

EDIBLE BOLETUS
(Boletus Edulis)

This mushroom has a distinctive sweet, nutty flavor. It dries well, and is often cooked in stews.

The cap is 2½-8 inches in diameter, convex when young, flattening as it matures; it is covered with a sticky-slimy skin (when moist) light tan to brown in color; sometimes the skin needs to be peeled off for eating. The pores are white to pale yellowish-green and they should be cut off before cooking. The spores are olive brown. The stem is 2½-6 inches long, thick and swollen at the base, and marked with a network of slightly raised veins. (Mid-July to September)

Wild animals seem to like the Boletus best of all the mushrooms. Humans enjoy them too, and so do insects. It is difficult to obtain mature specimens which are free from insect larvae, so they are best picked in the young button stage.

PICKING MUSHROOMS

Bring along a little brush (a pastry brush will do) and a knife. Cut off ends to avoid getting dirt in your basket.

Pick only fresh, young mushrooms. Never mix unknown species with edible ones; it is best to leave any mushroom that you don't know strictly alone. When you get home, brush the mushrooms, wash if necessary, and dry them. Try to use them on the day they are picked. Cooked mushrooms will keep for several days in the refrigerator; otherwise, dry, can or freeze them.

DRYING MUSHROOMS

To dry mushrooms, thread them onto a string, or lay them out on paper towels or on a screen, and keep them in a place that is free from moisture. When well dried out, they can be kept in sealed, sterilized glass jars.

As an added precaution against spoilage, boil mushrooms in water for 3 minutes before drying them.

When you want to use the dried mushrooms, soak them in warm water for several hours, and cook in stews, in gravy, in sauces or in soup.

WILD DRIED MUSHROOMS

Soak the dried mushrooms for 1 hour in dry white wine. Add these to the regular cultivated variety of mushrooms. (The flavor of the commercial mushrooms will be improved by the addition of the wild mushrooms.) This mixture can be used in any mushroom dish.

FREEZING MUSHROOMS

The little button mushrooms may be frozen whole and unpeeled.

Wipe mushrooms with paper towels to clean. Put 1 pint mushrooms into 1 pint water with 3 teaspoons lemon juice so that they won't darken.

Just before freezing remove mushrooms from lemon juice and water, and scald them in a pot of boiling water for 2 or 3 minutes. Cool mushrooms in ice water for as long as it takes for the blanching, 2 or 3 minutes. Drain, wrap and freeze.

GIANT PUFFBALL
(Calvatia Gigantea)

The giant puffball grows 8-12 inches in diameter or more, in the shape of a round or oval ball, attached to the ground by a cord-like root. The young puffball is white and smooth outside, and white and firm inside. This is the only time that it is good eating. Later it turns brown, and begins to break open at the top. The inside dries up and turns yellow and soggy. Do not eat a puffball that is at all yellow. When it reaches a stage where it has turned to a dark olive brown, the inside has dried out to a powder and is then very toxic.

PUFFBALL STEAKS

Cut puffball into slices. Dip in beaten egg and roll in bread crumbs. Fry, and drain before serving.

ORANGE DELICIOUS
(Lactarius Deliciosus)

The cap is 3-6 inches across; as it matures the edges become raised giving it a somewhat depressed center. It is pale to deep orange, and usually has greenish stains or spots, later fading to grayish or gray-green. The stem is 1½-4 inches long, and ½-1 inch thick. The flesh is white, but appears orange, because of the reddish-orange juice which seeps out when the flesh, gills or stems are cut or broken. The juice later turns greenish. Carefully note the color and flavor of the juice; it should be mild to taste, and should be orange.

WILD BERRIES

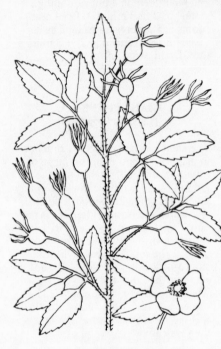

ROSE HIPS
(Rosa acicularis)

The wild rose grows on prickly bushes 2-5 feet high. The flowers are a delicate pink, sometimes a deep, dark rose. In August or September, after the seed pods have been nipped by frost, they are red and soft, and ready to be picked.

Three or four rose hips contain as much vitamin C as one orange. They'll keep well in the freezer, or dried; or they can be eaten right off the bushes all during the winter.

FRESH ROSE HIPS

Remove seeds and fluff from center of rose hips. Cut into halves and combine with an assortment of fresh fruits; sliced bananas, grapes, strawberries and oranges will give you a good basis for a compote. Squeeze orange juice over the fruit to moisten; stir in a little honey if the fruit isn't sweet enough.

ROSE HIP PUREE

Method 1:
> 1 pound rose hips
>   or half rose hips and half
>   low-bush cranberries, or
>   cut-up cooking apples
> 3 cups water

Cut open rose hips, and simmer in water for about 30 minutes, or until soft; the low-bush cranberries, if used, can be added the last 15 minutes.

Press berries through a sieve; sweeten puree to taste, and stir in a little lemon juice; it will help to preserve vitamin C as well as to add tartness.

Method 2:
The rose hips may be cleaned before cooking them. This is a very tedious task, but it does make a better tasting puree. (If you use this method the puree may be made in the blender.)

Method 3:
Gather well-ripened berries, and spread out in a dry, shady place to fully ripen.

When berries are nice and soft, rub them through a sieve with a wooden spoon. Sweeten puree to taste. (Leftover skin and pulp may be dried for tea.)

ROSE HIP JAM

> 4 pounds rose hip puree
> brown sugar to taste
> juice of 2 lemons

Combine ingredients and put over low heat; boil down to a thick consistency. Pour into jars and seal, or keep in refrigerator.

ROSE HIP RAISINS

Cut berries open; remove center, fluff and seeds. Spread out in a shallow pan.

Dry in a very slow oven (about 200 F) or in a warm dry place, or in a kettle placed at the edge of a campfire.

ROSE HIP–CRANBERRY PUDDING

The tart low-bush cranberry complements the blandness of the rose hip and imparts a rich red color to the pudding.

4 cups cranberry and rose hip puree, sweetened to taste
2 tablespoons cornstarch or potato starch
3 tablespoons cold water

Bring puree to a boil.

Dissolve starch in the cold water, and stir into the boiling puree. Cook for about 3 minutes, or until thickened, stirring constantly. Pour into large serving dish or into individual dishes, and serve warm or cold.

(Raspberry puree may be used instead of cranberry-rose hip puree.)

CANDIED ROSE HIPS

Simmer cleaned rose hips in a syrup made with water and honey, for 10 minutes. Drain on waxed paper. Dry in a very slow oven. Store between sheets of waxed paper. (Can be used in cookies, in fruitcake and in puddings.)

Or preserve fresh cleaned rose hips in honey to cover.

ROSE HIP TEA

1-1½ teaspoons dried rose hips
1 cup boiling water

Put boiling water into tea pot or cup and add rose hips. Cover and let stand 10 minutes. Serve with lemon and honey.

ROSE HIP DRINK

Make rose hip tea, and let it steep until cold. Strain; stir in a little lemon juice, and sweeten to taste.

LOW-BUSH CRANBERRY, or LINGONBERRY (Vaccinium vitis ideae)

The low-bush cranberry, also known as the mountain cranberry or lingonberry, grows profusely in bogs or spruce-covered areas. The leaves are leathery, on creeping stems 1-6 inches high; the flowers are pale pink.

The berries are ready to pick in August, just before the first frosts; they are smaller than, but similar to, the commercial cranberry, and can be prepared the same way.

CRANBERRY JUICE

6 cups cranberries
1 teaspoon lemon juice

Simmer cranberries in enough water to cover, until the skins pop open. Strain juice; stir in lemon juice, and sweeten to taste.

HOT CRANBERRY PUNCH

cranberry juice
apple juice, orange juice, or pineapple juice (optional)
cinnamon sticks

Combine juices; heat; serve in mugs with a stick of cinnamon in each, or instead of the cinnamon, a thin slice of lemon studded with 3 allspice berries.

CRANBERRY CATSUP

2½ pounds low-bush cranberries
   (8 cups)
1 cup vinegar
2 cups brown sugar
1 cup water
2 tablespoons cinnamon
Cook cranberries in vinegar until they
burst open.
   Add sugar, water and cinnamon,
and boil down to desired thickness.
Seal in sterilized jars.

Variation:

Add ¾-1 teaspoon ground allspice.
Rose hip puree may be used in place of
or in combination with the cranberries.

CRANBERRY-ORANGE RELISH

4 cups raw cranberries
2 large oranges
1½ cups honey
Remove peel, seeds and white segments
from oranges. Grind cranberries and
oranges in food chopper; mix well with
honey. Serve cold. (Makes 1 quart.)

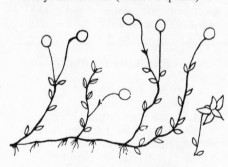

SWAMP CRANBERRY
(Oxycoccus microcarpus)

The flowers are deep pink, on thread-
like, creeping stems. The tiny, leathery
leaves are dark green above, and whitish
underneath; the berry is red. It can be
found trailing through moss, in swamps
or bogs.
   This is a very sour berry; it is used
to make sauce, jelly or juice.

CRANBERRY SAUCE

Simmer cranberries in a small amount
of water until they begin to pop open.
Sweeten with honey to taste.

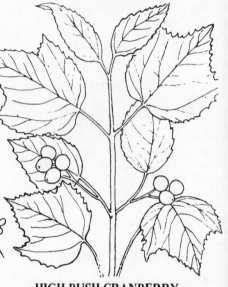

HIGH BUSH CRANBERRY,
MOOSEBERRY, SQUASHBERRY
(Viburnum edule)

The bushes are 1-4 feet high, and they
grow in moist, shaded woods and
thickets. The leaves are olive-green,
and the flowers are white.
   The berries when ripe are light red,
with a large stone inside; they are best
made into juice or jelly.

CRANBERRY JELLY

Put berries into pan with enough water
so that you just see it through the
fruit, or about 1 part water to 2 parts
berries. Simmer until soft enough to
mash; strain. The first dripping makes
a clear jelly; the second dripping is put
through a sieve and made into jam.
   For each cup of juice add ¾ cup
sugar;* the sugar should be warmed
in the oven beforehand. Boil mixture
until it forms 1 large drop or sheet on
the spoon, 8-30 minutes.

*Raw sugar may be used.

INDIAN ICE CREAM

Put 1 tablespoon of soapberries into a big bowl (there musn't be a bit of grease in it). Mash berries with 2 tablespoons water and 1 tablespoon sugar or honey. Beat until very thick and frothy, and almost white, adding a little more water as you beat.

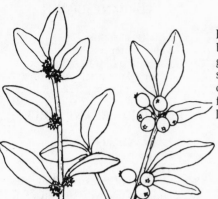

SOAPBERRY or SOAPOLLALIE
(Shepherdia canadensis)

The soapberry bush grows 3-6 feet high in open woods. The flowers are pale yellow, and the leaves are green on top, silvery underneath.

The berries are orange-red, sweet, acid and aromatic; they look like rose hips, and similarly, they are sweeter after the first frost.

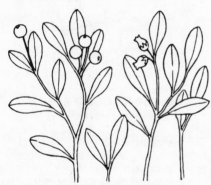

KINNIKINNICK or MEALBERRY
(Arctostaphylos uva ursi)

Kinnikinnick grows in open, wooded areas in rocky, sandy ground. The flowers are white or pink-tinged, on a low trailing shrub with firm, lustrous leaves.

The berries are red, with a large stone, consisting of several nutlets inside. The flesh is sparse, dry and mealy. It can be made into a beverage by steeping the berries in boiling tea.

KINNIKINNICK TEA

Pour a little hot tea (any kind) over Kinnikinnick berries; beat and mush to extract juice. Strain, and add more tea, or dilute with water.

RED BEARBERRY
(Arctostaphylos rubra)

The red bearberry is a little larger than the black bearberry, and it grows in woods, at lower elevations.

The flowers are pink or white, and later on in the fall, when the flowers have been replaced by juicy, scarlet berries, the leaves turn to bright red.

NORTHERN BLACK CURRANT
(Ribes hudsonianum)

The berries are black, and the flowers are white; they grow on a bush 1-3 feet high, in moist woods and along streams.

The raw berry is a little bitter; the flavor is improved when it is diluted with water and made into juice or jelly. After the juice is strained, the remaining pulp can be used to make jam.

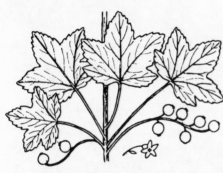

NORTHERN RED CURRANT
(Ribes triste)

This is a low sprawling bush, found in mossy woods and boggy places. The leaves are light green above, somewhat pale white and woolly underneath; the flowers are brownish to purplish.

The berries are bright red and sour, but good to eat. They are usually made into juice, jelly or pudding.

CURRANT JUICE

2 quarts currants
3 cups water

Crush currants; add water. Simmer, covered, for 10 minutes. Pour into a jelly bag or cloth to squeeze out juice.

ROSE HIP CURRANT SYRUP

2 cups currants
2 cups rose hips
2 cups dates

Clean rose hips of seeds and fluff, pit dates, and combine with currants. Put through food chopper, or puree in blender. Add water if a thinner consistency is desired.

Variation:

Omit dates. Soak 2 cups raisins in 2 cups water for several days; drain off juice and boil down to 1 cup. Mix the hot raisin syrup with the pureed rose hips and currants. This syrup is very rich in vitamin C; keep in a cold place, and/or seal in sterilized jars.

NORTHERN GOOSEBERRY
(Ribes oxyacanthoides)

The gooseberry bush grows 1½-3 feet high, in moist places. The flowers are greenish-white or purplish.

Gooseberries are palatable in the greenish-purple and off-white stage, before they are completely ripe. Ripe, they are a reddish-purple, sweet but mushy.

GOOSEBERRY SAUCE

Pick both nearly-ripe and fully-ripe gooseberries, and simmer with a little water for about 7 minutes. Sweeten to taste, preferably with honey.

BLACK BEARBERRY
(Arctostaphylos alpina)

This is a trailing shrub, usually found growing in the mountains. The leaves are wrinkled and veiny, and the flowers are pinkish-white. The berries, when ripe, are purple-black and juicy but insipid. The taste is improved by cooking.

WILD RED RASPBERRY
(Rubus idaeus)

The fruit is light red, juicy, and pleasant to taste.

It can be found in scattered patches in open woods and on mountain slopes, on bushes 2-6 feet high. The flowers are white.

RASPBERRY LEAF TEA

Steep a scant teaspoon dried raspberry leaves in 1 cup boiling water for 3 minutes.

BERRY PUDDING

Simmer equal parts red raspberries and red currants in enough water to cover, until the fruit is soft and has begun to lose its color.

Strain berries, and sweeten juice to taste.

For each quart of juice mix 3 teaspoons potato starch or cornstarch with a few tablespoons cold water; stir this into the juice.

Boil, stirring constantly, until the starch is cooked and the pudding begins to thicken. Serve warm or cold.

If you don't have red currants, substitute cranberries or other tart berries —whatever is available.

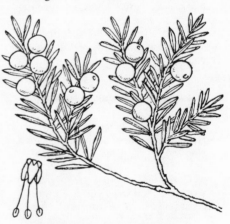

MOSSBERRY or CROWBERRY
(Empetrum nigrum)

The berries are black and juicy with 6-9 hard seeds inside; they grow on a trailing evergreen shrub in cold, sandy, rocky places. The flowers are pinkish or purplish.

After the first frost, the berries become sweeter; before it they must be mixed with blueberries and made into pie or preserves.

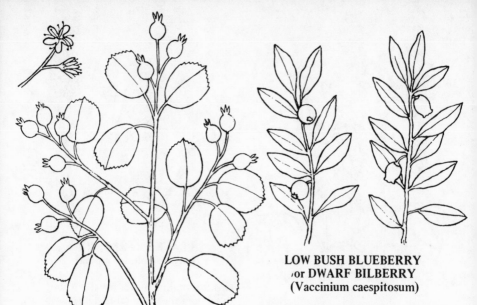

LOW BUSH BLUEBERRY or DWARF BILBERRY
(Vaccinium caespitosum)

The berries are light blue with a whitish bloom, growing on shrubs 2-12 inches high, on gravelly shores and in wooded areas. The leaves are lustrous green and thin, and the flowers are pink.

The flavor is sweet, and excellent raw or cooked.

SERVICEBERRY or SASKATOON
(Amelanchier alnifolia)

The berries when ripe are purplish-black, sweet and juicy; they are eaten raw or cooked.

The bushes grow 3-5 feet high, in sandy, rocky wooded areas and open country. The flowers are white.

PRESERVING WILD BERRIES

Wild berries will keep well in the ground. Dig a hole deep enough for a wooden barrel, place barrel in the hole and fill with berries. Cover with a weighted lid, and year-round you can scoop out berries as you need them. Glass jars or crocks can also be used.

Berries to be frozen in a home freezer may be put into plastic bags, wrapped securely and frozen. Thaw in a cold place preferably, and use for puddings, sauces, compotes or baked dishes.

A simple way to dry wild berries is to spread them out on a white sheet in the sun. Shake sheet to turn berries. When dry, hang them up in porous sacks to keep. When you wish to use them, soak berries in water for about an hour.

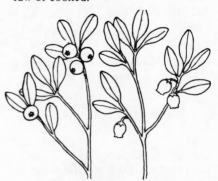

BOG BLUEBERRY or BILBERRY
(Vaccinium uliginosum)

The berries are bluish-black with a whitish bloom; the leaves are thick, and they grow on shrubs 6-12 inches high, in bogs, along lake shores, and on hillsides and mountain summits. The flowers are pink.

They are eaten raw, boiled, or baked in sourdough pancakes, bannock, muffins and pie.

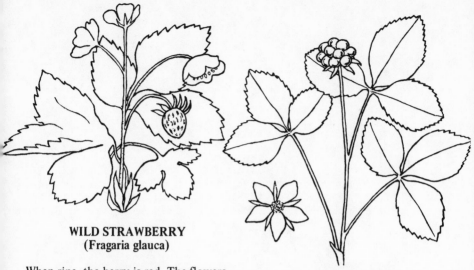

WILD STRAWBERRY
(Fragaria glauca)

When ripe, the berry is red. The flowers are white, and the plants grow 3-4 inches high, in meadows and open areas. Usually the berry is eaten raw.

NAGOONBERRY, or
ARCTIC ROSEBERRY
(Rubus arcticus)

The berries grow 4-10 inches high, in cool, mossy thickets and swamps, in meadows and near creeks. They are dark red, and look like raspberries. The flowers are deep rose-red.

SILVERBERRY
(Elaeagnus commutata)

These silver-colored berries are dry and mealy, with a stone inside.

They grow on a bush, 4-12 feet high, with dark, grayish-red branches and silvery scruffy leaves. The flowers are silvery outside and yellowish inside.

CLOUDBERRY, or
BAKED APPLE BERRY
(Rubus chamaemorus)

This is a sweet, golden-amber colored berry, found in peat bogs and muskeg. It grows 2-6 inches high, and the flower is white.

57

Contributors

Mr. and Mrs. Howard Firth
Belle Desrosiers
Sylvia Williams
Mr. R.T. Porsild
Mr. A.E. Porsild
Gertie Tom
Dora Wedge
Jean Jamieson
Ron Chambers
Tagish Anne
Allen Innes-Taylor
Charlie and Betty Taylor
Dr. J.V. Clark
Mrs. Berent Hougen
Mrs. J.O. Erickson
Dr. Pugh
Rose Page
John Harach
Henri Gall
Charlotte Williams
Victoria Faulkner
Mrs. Rolph Bailey
Delores Cline Brown
Grace Chambers
George Edzerza
Mary Jeckle
Jim Robb
Margrette Gaundroue
Mary Taylor

Sue Van Bibber
Marne Drury
Curly Desrosiers
Barbara Currie
Lynn Ramage
Onni Lahikainen
Paul Mann
Kitty Bungerz
Toots Smoler
Flo Vars
Mrs. Archie Bruce
Mr. C.W. Craig
Mrs. George Jeckel
Martha Louise Black
Mrs. F.H. Osborn Sr.
Mrs. W.D. McKay
Ellen Schofield
June Adams
Betty Buffet
Martha Cameron
Zoe Cousins
Ione Christenson
Barbara Baker
Lucy Wren
Walter Wauhkonen
George Peel
Jeanne Harbottle
Chef Nelson Lewis

INDEX

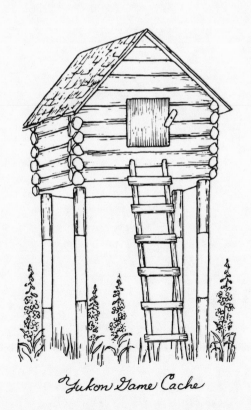

Yukon Game Cache